GEORGE RYLAND

APOSTLE

TIME
FOR
TONGUES

Time for Tongues

Published by Ryland Books
P O Box 1461, Mulbarton, Johannesburg, 2059
admin@ryland-publications.co.za

ISBN 978-0-620-83989-1

All scripture references are taken from the New King James Version of the Bible unless otherwise stated.

Cover photograph by Jess Sterk Photography
Cover concept by Calynn Hefke
Layout by Boutique Books
Printed in South Africa by Digital Action

Time for Tongues
is
dedicated to

my wife
Ruth Maude

– whom I love dearly and forever –

for the deep inspiration that she
gave to this book

CONTENTS

PREFACE

There is a time and a season for every purpose in the fabric of God's grand scheme of things. Every phase of His plan and purpose for the church is ushered in by the Lord Jesus Christ Himself.

There was a time when our Lord brought back to this world the knowledge of saving faith. Before that, many people thought that their good works could save them. God, in His wonderful wisdom and mercy, restored the knowledge of saving faith to the church. Today it is commonplace for people to preach that the just shall live by faith.

For a very long time, people thought that sprinkling babies in water was baptism. There came a time when God dismissed this ignorance and restored the knowledge of immersion to the church. Today, full immersion in water is standard practice. The time for the restoration of that truth was then. The same applied to holiness, to healing, to teaching, to prosperity and to deliverance. There was a time and a season for the restoration of each of these truths to the Body of Christ.

It was not long after the first century that the truths mentioned above came under severe attack from workers of darkness. These false teachers deliberately introduced false doctrines into churches to hinder the progress of the true church. False churches arose that taught damnable heresies. This is what pushed the church into the dark ages.

The same happened to the gifts of the Holy Spirit, and in particular tongues.

However, in God's work of restoration He brought about two similar moves of the Spirit during the last century. First came the Pentecostal move at the beginning of the twentieth century and then came the Charismatic move that began near the end of the 1950s.

During these times there were many manifestations of the gifts of the Spirit. There was much speaking in tongues, but this soon faded out. Pastors got scared that speaking in tongues would cause trouble and people would leave their churches. They subsequently invented doctrines to try and curb what they thought was wild fire. These wet blankets were responsible for snuffing out the flames. After a while the church was left with only a spattering of tongues here and there. God is dismissing this ignorance now, because the very issue that God told the church not to be ignorant about is precisely the issue around which gross ignorance abounds.

The Lord is now ushering in a time for tongues. This time is bringing forth a new and a fresh revelation of tongues. Knowledge of what tongues can accomplish is breaking forth into circles of Spirit-filled believers. More and more people are realizing that this is the hour for tongues, and it is a time to learn more about the gift.

We must embrace this time for tongues with bold faith. When an effectual spiritual door opens, believers must step through boldly, doubting nothing. A door shuts on those who reject His beckoning invitation. If we want to discover the power of tongues, we must enter in. This season should not be despised.

Then, just as the gift of tongues is the gateway to the other gifts of the Holy Spirit, so is this time for tongues a gateway to a time for the other gifts of the Spirit. There will be a time for each in God's plan of restoration. Greater and more glorious times are coming. There is a time coming that will bring in the very glory of the manifestation of the sons of God who now walk incognito in this world. This will lead to the manifest glory of the Most High being displayed for all to see.

Beloved, it is time for tongues. It is time to yield to praying at length in tongues. It is time for focused praying in tongues. It is time for concerted praying in tongues. It is time for prevailing praying in tongues. It is time for knowledgeable praying in tongues. It is time for victorious praying in tongues. It is time for the power of tongues. It is time for tongues.

INTRODUCTION

This book is about the many benefits that praying at length in tongues brings, the scriptural basis for the gift, and an exposé of false doctrines. I am certain that there is much more that can be written about the gift, but hopefully what has been set down on paper will help propel you in the right direction.

Praying at length in tongues is praying for long stretches of time in tongues. This is explained in this book as two or more hours of private praying in tongues. It includes praying in tongues when taking walks, driving, flying, working at home and whenever alone. Short bursts of tongues here and there do not fall under this definition.

Those who pray at length in tongues give God the opportunity to express His great love for them in tangible ways. He does this through His divine order of doing things. As long as Spirit-filled believers pray at length in tongues, remain plugged in every day, yield to Him, keep on stirring up the gift and maintain the fullness of the Spirit, they can expect the blessings to flow. The limits on God will be removed and His plans and purposes for their lives will progress. It is praying for long periods of time in tongues that produces the blessings of God and proves what power praying like this brings. Read and discover all the other blessings that praying at length in tongues produces.

There is a solid scriptural basis for praying in tongues. Tongues is an interesting subject and is found in both the Old and New Testament scriptures. Careful study will prove that tongues is for today and will produce confidence in the believer to pursue the will of God in this regard. Every Spirit-filled believer must know how to operate in the gift according to scriptural parameters.

The gift of Different Kinds of Tongues is a powerful gift and has not escaped the attention of the wicked one. He desires and works to snuff it out. In the past he has found willing vessels who have done his will and have twisted the Word. Those who rightly divide the Word of Truth must show believers what the scriptures really teach. The believer must be solidly based in the truth to be safeguarded, to be able to stand against and to overcome all the wiles of the devil.

Important to remember is that this book is written in such a manner that, after the first reading, chapters and portions thereof can be revisited for study and meditation. This will result in the Spirit-filled believer being established in the knowledge of the gift and the scriptures.

A short guide on how to be saved and a sinner's prayer is given at the end of the book. Anyone who is not saved can follow these instructions and if he or she prays the prayer with all sincerity they will be saved. Guidance on how to receive the Baptism in the Holy Spirit is also given.

References to various scriptures are given throughout the book. If readers open their bibles and search these scriptures out, they will gain a wealth of knowledge and will get the full benefit of the book. If this book is read in its entirety, studied and acted upon, the reader's life will be changed forever.

FIRST THINGS FIRST

This book is written primarily for those who are already baptized in the Holy Spirit. The principles and exhortations given in this book must not be pursued by those who are not born again and by those who are not baptized in the Holy Spirit. Those who are not saved must first get saved and those who are not baptized in the Holy Spirit must first be filled with the Spirit. A short guide on how to get saved and how to be filled with the Spirit is given at the end of this book. Those who are not saved and those who are not baptized in the Holy Spirit must first follow the instructions given there before embarking on trying to appropriate the truths shared in this book.

PART ONE

THE POWER OF TONGUES

1 TONGUES

I turned to the Lord Jesus Christ on the 24th of June 1981. About three months after this greatest day of my life, I was invited to attend a believers' meeting that was to be held at somebody's home. I agreed to go and arrived there at about ten on that bright Saturday morning. We were about forty believers who had gathered in the spacious lounge. Somebody led the singing, another strummed a guitar and the rest of the people sang fervently. At a certain point during the worship there was a sudden hush and we all began to reverence the Lord.

Then, without any warning, somebody directly behind me broke out, speaking loudly in a language that was unknown to me. It was clear and fluent but one I had never heard before. I stiffened as I felt the power of God fill up the room. After the speaking subsided there was another hush. Although the almost tangible holy silence continued for just a few moments, it seemed to last forever. The fear of God filled the place.

What followed was equally astounding. Somebody else started speaking in English and it was obvious that the person was giving the gist of what had been said in the unknown language. After that there was a hush again, and then everybody broke out into praise and magnified the Lord in words, instruments and song. Thereafter a reverential presence prevailed as the appointed preacher ministered under a deepened anointing of the Holy Spirit.

I had never before experienced what had just happened, although I had heard a sprinkling of tongues here and there. After the meeting I enquired from a friend what it all had meant. He chuckled quietly and said that I sounded like the Jews in the second chapter of the Book of Acts who, perplexed after hearing the disciples speak in tongues, asked what all that had meant.

He then went on and explained to me that the woman who had spoken in the language that I did not understand had spoken in tongues, and the hush that I had felt was the people recognizing the presence of God. He continued by explaining to me that the English speaking after the hush was the interpretation of the tongues and the people's praising and magnifying God was a response to the divine Word.

After that experience I could not rest until I myself was filled with the Holy Spirit. I went up for every altar call that was made for those who wanted to be filled with the Holy Spirit, but I never spoke in tongues. A friend of mine told me that I was filled with the Holy Spirit because nobody would be able to preach like I did if he or she was not filled with the Holy Spirit.

I was not satisfied with this explanation. I wanted to be filled with the Holy Spirit with the evidence of speaking in other tongues as they had received in the Book of Acts.

Another brother said that I must have been filled with the Holy Spirit because I had such a zeal for the gospel. None of these explanations satisfied me. I wanted to be filled with the Holy Spirit with the initial evidence of speaking in other tongues.

I was super-thirsty to be filled. The scriptures had me locked in the desire to be filled with the Spirit and I could not get past the instructions of the Lord Jesus Christ.

LUKE 24:49 – *Behold, I send the Promise of My Father upon you; but tarry in the city of Jerusalem until you are endued with power from on high.*

ACTS 1:8 – *But you shall receive power when the Holy Spirit has come upon you; and you shall be witnesses to Me in Jerusalem, and in all Judea and Samaria, and to the end of the earth.*

One day, after I had finished praying in an early Sunday morning prayer meeting in November 1981, I sat in a corner chair and flipped the pages of the bible. When I reached the letter that Jude had written to believers I began to read. In my short time of salvation, I had read the entire New Testament, but the twentieth verse of the letter had not made any impression on me. However, that morning as I read, the verse came alive and sprang out of the pages, gripping my attention.

JUDE 1:20 – *But you, beloved, building yourselves up on your most holy faith, praying in the Holy Spirit.*

I was so excited and, immediately after the prayer meeting, I rushed to the believers asking them if they had ever seen the scripture before. Of course they had, but I thought that I was the first to discover it. I did not know that I had received divine illumination of inspired writing. Full of faith, I headed home to get ready for the morning service.

When I got to the service, which was being held in a school classroom, I joined the believers and we worshipped the Lord together. I got baptized in the Holy Spirit that morning and I remember the moment very clearly. I had my hands lifted up to heaven and was standing at the first seat on the left side of the third row facing the pulpit when the pastor came around to me and laid his hands on my head and prayed, "Father, anoint this young man to be an intercessor and a soul winner".

After he'd prayed that prayer, with my hands still lifted up to the throne of God, I praised God saying, "Hallelujah". After using this word in worship for the third time, words began to float up from deep down within me. When I spoke them out, I heard a clear, beautiful and flowery language emerge out of my mouth. I also had an incredible sense of standing in a vast wheat field somewhere far away in Israel and speaking a clear Hebrew language.

How long this continued, I don't know. What I do remember is that I heard people fall and crash into chairs all around me. After a while, as the words subsided, I stopped speaking. After the service someone took me home where I spent the rest of the afternoon thanking God for baptizing me in the Holy Spirit. I had received an Acts 2:4 experience, just as I had desired and pursued.

On the Wednesday evening following, I was in the weekly prayer meeting when I felt similar supernatural words, as had risen in me on the Sunday, rise up in my spirit again. I yielded by lifting up my voice and speaking the words out. Praise God, I spoke in tongues again as the Spirit gave me utterance. As had happened on the Sunday, I heard people falling under the power all over the room.

Although I was now settled and satisfied that I had been filled with the Holy Spirit, I did not speak in tongues again for about two months. One day a brother came alongside me and asked me why I had not spoken in tongues since I had been filled with the Holy Spirit. I answered him saying that I was waiting for the Holy Spirit to give me another experience as He had done on the previous two occasions. The man then informed me that it was not the Holy Spirit's responsibility to speak in tongues but mine and proceeded to instruct me on how to yield. I yielded and have been doing so ever since.

Continuing

After my baptism in the Holy Spirit I began to listen to and read after Holy Spirit-filled preachers along the lines of their teaching on praying in the Spirit. I gave myself to long sessions of praying in tongues and was on a roll when I began to pastor in 1983.

It is amazing how the church flourished. The altar calls were always filled with many souls as a great move of the Spirit began. We cast out demons and laid hands on the sick, getting many miracles. A bible school was soon opened, with many graduations in the years that followed. The church grew and we had awesome conventions with people coming from across the country to attend. New churches were spawned, giving impetus to the move of God. We had many supernatural manifestations of the Holy Spirit and experiences that I will share later on in this book. I was and am still convinced that the move of God was due to the long stretches of praying in tongues.

Ruth and I got married in 1997 and we both submerged ourselves in the work of God. The church grew further, and other branches were started. However, the Lord had a different plan for us. The huge army that was around us would not be the ones to go into battle with us in the future. Like Gideon's army, we were reduced to but a handful.

This happened in 2003 when we entered into a great struggle. At that time we reached a point that we can only describe as 'rock bottom'. Our prosperous church had been reduced to but a few people. We barely made it through each day. Whatever we attempted just never seemed to work out for us. We had very little and struggled along. I really don't know how we got to church with our struggling, stuttering and stalling car. Many times I wondered how we could have made it through each day. Many were saying, "George is finished," and I myself saw no way out. This continued for a number of years. In 2008 we were still hopping along.

One day, in great anguish, I cried out to the Lord saying, "Help us, Lord. Speak to me or speak to my wife. We need a word from You."

The promise of the Lord is, "Call upon Me in the day of trouble and I will deliver you, and you shall glorify Me" (Ps. 50:15). I did and, while I was still crying out to the Lord, my wife, who was on the other side of the house, heard the audible voice of the Lord say, "Pray in tongues for two hours every day". This was our deliverance. I now know what the singer meant when he penned these words to his song: "We need a word from You, Lord". All we needed was but one word from the Lord, and we got it. Hallelujah!

Up to that time we did pray in tongues. However, we did not have structured praying in tongues for two hours every. We missed our praying times as we pleased. Now we obeyed God and things began to change, and within four years we, who had had so little that we could hardly make it to church, were traveling the length and the breadth of the United States of America, preaching the gospel of Jesus Christ.

Our praying in tongues and obedience did not only upgrade our prosperity, it also moved us into God's plan and purpose for our lives. We started discovering His will for us and what a surprise that was. Things also began to change in our church as the Lord stabilized it and gave it growth. Demonic forces were overcome and witches that were set against us were exposed and driven away by the power of the Holy Spirit.

Tongues did and still does it for us. We know that it is tongues and cannot be convinced otherwise. We are more persuaded day by day as God teaches us more about the power of tongues.

Deliverance for All

This praying at length in tongues is not only for us, and for the many that the Lord has already started on the path to victory. It is also for the entire Body of Christ. He desires to bring them all into His move. This is for each one's benefit, for the progress of the church, the defeat of the wicked one and for His glory. So, the Lord wants more and more people to join in praying at length in tongues. All should avail themselves to be added to this mighty army. Another thousand must be added, and another thousand, until there are millions upon millions and even billions of spiritual mouths that have been opened and are praying in tongues. Think about it: billions of believers becoming polished arrows, shot into this world from the bow of the Heavenly Archer. In every community where these believers are, open heavens will develop in the spirit world and long-standing religions, traditions of men, will come tumbling down and a multitude of souls will be saved. It is no wonder that the devil wants to silence tongues.

Deliverance and victory is for you too. You will get there when you discover His plan and purpose and follow hard after it. The Father loves you and wants to do it for you.

2 THE FATHER'S LOVE

Smoking Flax/Bruised Reed

Deliverance and victory is for you, but let's first pause here and consider the wonderful love of God. Tongues is the conduit for bringing this love into manifestation in your life.

The Father loves you with an eternal, unchanging love. You should never lose sight of that. He does not love you with some special love that is reserved for mere human beings, but He loves you with the same love with which He loves His very own Son. Think about that. As the Father loves the Son, so does He love you. The Lord Jesus Christ Himself prayed that the Father would reveal this to those who believed in Him.

JOHN 17:23 – *I in them, and You in Me; that they may be made perfect in one, and that the world may know that You have sent Me, and have loved them as You have loved Me.*

Nobody will ever be able to fathom the depths of God's awesome love. Human thought, however stretched, cannot plumb even a minute iota of the knowledge of His glorious love. In this life we see but dimly, as through a mirror. We must wait for eternity before we will know, even as we shall be known. Only the Holy Spirit can reveal God's love to us, and He does so in the ultimate revelation of it in the Book of John.

JOHN 3:16 – *For God so loved the world that He gave His only begotten Son, that whoever believes in Him should not perish but have everlasting life.*

Think about His awesome love for you. The Father sent His only begotten Son to die in your place. He drew you to the cross and, when you believed in His Son, He gave you the full package of salvation. He never stopped there but sent His very own Spirit to dwell in you. Isn't that utterly amazing love?

Now, if He gave us His Son and gave us the Holy Spirit, how is it ever possible that He could withhold any good thing from us? Never! All things are ours (1 Cor. 3:21-22). Full provision for all our needs, desires and wants has been made. The Father has not only given us all things, but He also wants us to freely enjoy it all (Rom. 8:32 and 1 Tim. 6:17).

Now consider this aspect of His love. Every human being is so special and so unique in the sight of God that, before the world was ever created, He already had a perfect plan and a perfect purpose for each one of them. The glory of this plan cannot, even in the smallest degree, be matched by anyone's most unbridled imagination. He loves each one so much that all His thoughts about them are continuously for their welfare, for their peace and for their full and blessed final outcome (Jer. 29:11).

Now, I ask you, can the Father Who loves us so much, Who has done all that He has done for us, and Who has a perfect plan and purpose for each one of us, just leave you to struggle through life without any help from Him? Would He do that to you? No! Never! On the contrary, He is on His throne, ever shuddering and bursting forth with overflowing desire to bless you exceedingly abundantly above all that you could ever ask, think or imagine. He desires to extricate you from all the swamps of life.

No matter how bad the situation is, how deep your suffering is, how hopelessly you flounder about, the Father wants and desires to deliver you. Yes, even if you are on the lowest rung, He wants to give you supernatural assistance so that you can climb up the ladder again. However bad the quagmire is, the Father wants to free you, and that with extraordinary speed. Our loving heavenly Father can and is willing to do so. He will never quench a smoking flax and He will never break a bruised reed (Matt. 12:20). The question is, "How does He do it?"

Stuck in the Mud

There are a lot of things that can keep you stuck in the mud. Ignorance or neglecting to walk in the God-kind of life, ignoring or not knowing the divine way of doing things, thinking that the onus for your prosperity is on God and generally pursuing the wind will all prevent you from moving in God's plan and purpose for your life.

If you are ignorant of how, or you neglect, to walk in the God-kind of life, you will lose out on the blessings that come directly from the throne. No matter how consecrated you are, you might not realize that you are confining the outcome of your life to the lower life that sinners live. The God-kind of life is the abundant life that the Lord Jesus Christ spoke of when He was upon the earth (John 10:10). The lower kind of life is only walking under the loving-kindness of God. The Lord taught on this in His discourse on the Mount.

MATTHEW 5:45 – *That you may be sons of your Father in heaven; for He makes His sun rise on the evil and on the good and sends rain on the just and on the unjust.*

The Father is good to all. The sun rises every morning for the benefit of all creation and the rain falls on believers, unbelievers and even haters of God. The lovingkindness of God extends to all human beings. Everything that He has created can be enjoyed by all those who live upon the earth. Humans make business out of the wind, gravity, trees, cattle, birds, rivers, seas, electricity, sound, light and from all other God-given things.

If you only rely on the lovingkindness of God, you will only prosper according to the prosperity of your country, your own aptitude and your own drive. Just as the sinner has potential to advance, so will you have potential to advance. It will be extremely hard, if not impossible, for you to get out of the swamps of life if you operate only according to your own abilities. The added difficulty is that the flesh, the devil and the world is against you.

Remaining ignorant of the divine order of doing things will keep you stuck in the mud. There can be very little change in your life if you are not educated in this regard. Even the most deeply dedicated Christian, who knows the scriptures and prays fervently in his or her learned language, can never pull their feet out of the miry clay if they ignore the workings of the divine Trinity.

You are deceived if you think and believe that, because God loves you, all that is necessary on your part is for you to wait for Him to move on your behalf. Such thinking comes from the wicked one. He delights in blocking believers from receiving on a supernatural basis by making them think that the onus is on God. The truth is, all things have been provided for them, but they must have an aggressive approach to the Word of God. It is their responsibility to possess the land that God has already graciously given them.

MATTHEW 11:12 – *And from the days of John the Baptist until now the kingdom of heaven suffers violence, and the violent take it by force.*

There are other areas of deception that distract believers from victory. An example is the belief in generational curses. Some believers have been convinced that curses that were put on their great-great-grandfathers are still effective in their lives and this blocks their prosperity. They think that they will never see a breakthrough in their lives until these curses have been broken by themselves or someone else.

Believers don't have to worry about this because there is no such teaching in the bible. What is written is that "Christ has redeemed us from the curse of the law having become a curse for us" (Gal. 3:13-14). If He redeemed us from the curse of the law, it cannot be that He left other curses unattended to. The precious blood of Jesus Christ is sufficient, having broken all bondages. Don't be troubled along these lines any further. Go for the genuine thing.

If you want to be set on the path to victory, do the following things. First, decide to pray at length in tongues and do it. Second, believe that the Word of God promises you the abundant life and act on the scriptures that relate to that. Third, take cognizance of the fact that there is a divine order of doing things and follow hard after it. Fourth, move forward with aggressive faith, fearing nothing. Fifth, consign all deceptive thinking to the bin, and do not go back to scratching around for those thoughts again because you are not a spiritual hobo. If these thought patterns try to come back, just say, "Oh no, I don't think like that anymore!"

Do these things and your forward movement will be evident for all to see.

3 THE NEED FOR TONGUES

Awesome Gift

Our heavenly Father needs us to pray at length in tongues in order for Him to deal with the devil on our behalf, to lift us out of the doldrums of life, to guide us into His plan and purpose for our lives and to drive the church forward into His glory. Praying in the understanding has its place, but by itself will only accomplish a minute percentage of what God wants to do.

Tongues is an extremely powerful gift of the Holy Spirit. What is regarded as the simple gift of tongues by many people is really the awesome gift of tongues. Every word spoken in tongues is a direct utterance of the Divine Mind and will always bring the tremendous power of God onto the scene. There is no word that comes from the Divine Mind that is devoid of power. Each is more explosive than a trillion nuclear explosions put together.

Luke 1:37 (Amplified) – *For with God nothing is ever impossible and no word from God shall be without power or impossible of fulfilment.*

The Father knows that when Spirit-filled believers pray in tongues, they are not activating some teeny-weeny spirit. The Spirit is a co-equal person in the triune Godhead and when He begins to move there are awful and unwelcome consequences for the devil. The shock waves, earthquakes, mighty rushing winds that are caused by the activity of the Greater One reverberate throughout the realm of darkness (1 John 4:4). Do not underestimate tongues.

There is nothing foolish about tongues at all. The Father has reserved this gift for all those who would live under a new and better covenant that is established on better promises. To those who are perishing, speaking in tongues is absolute foolishness, but to us who are filled with the Holy Spirit it brings the manifested power of God onto the scene.

Unfortunately, the majority of those who are saved hold the same opinion that the unsaved have about tongues. They would rather lean on the arm of flesh. Despite what the unsaved and the unlearned think, God moves ahead and through 'the foolishness of tongues' destroys the wisdom of the wise and brings to nothing the endeavours of those who consider themselves prudent. They profess themselves to be wise, but in that very professing they make themselves fools.

No argument or high thing that tries to exalt itself above the wisdom of God can stand before tongue-praying believers. The Father uses the foolishness of their tongues to confound the devil, to extricate the believer from all difficulties, to bring into effect His plan and purpose for His people and to propel the church into the fullness of His glory.

---

1 CORINTHIANS 1:27-29 – *But God has chosen the foolish things of the world to put to shame the wise, and God has chosen the weak things of the world to put to shame the things which are mighty; and the base things of the world and the things which are despised God has chosen,*

and the things which are not, to bring to nothing the things that are, that no flesh should glory in His presence.

Although, to a great many Christians, speaking in tongues is an embarrassment, to the devil the mere mention of it grips his heart with fear. He is terrified of what tongues can accomplish. What happened to his realm in the days of the Book of Acts, when Spirit-filled believers prayed at length in tongues, is still fresh in his memory. He gets nightmares when he thinks about the times throughout the ages, when great awakenings broke out and multitudes got saved as a result of men and women yielding to the Spirit and praying in tongues for extended periods of time. He has no fear at all if believers come against him in their own strength because he knows that it is not by might, nor by power, but only by the Spirit of God that he can be dislodged from his strongholds (Zech. 4:6).

The devil's ultimate fear is a manifestation of the Spirit of God. Speaking in tongues is one such manifestation and this proves that the kingdom of God is in operation. Satan knows that demonic powers can only be dealt with by the Holy Spirit (Luke 11:20), so he tries to block all speaking in tongues. The way he does this is by sending false teachers into churches to teach error. He has silenced whole denominations from speaking in tongues using this strategy.

His workers are always hard at work trying to block sinners from getting saved and, if they do get saved, they try to block these new believers from being baptized in the Holy Spirit. If they fail on that, they try to keep these Spirit-baptized believers from praying at length in tongues. If they do speak in tongues, they try to suppress it by convincing these believers that a spattering of tongues here and there is spirituality.

However, terror strikes their hearts if anyone gets a revelation of the power of tongues and begins to pray at length in the Spirit. Past experience has taught them that, if this is allowed and more and more people fall in line, it will lead to their total demise. So, they try to block all talk of tongues. They know that the seemingly great and invincible ruler of darkness will be brought down if believers begin to pray in tongues in great numbers throughout the world.

The time for tongues has arrived, and the ushering in of this time has also ushered in the imminent defeat of the dragon.

The Father needs us to pray at length in tongues so that He can deal with these things that affect us. Praying in the understanding has its role, but for now it suffices to say that it is but a learned human language to communicate with those around us. Speaking in tongues is a heavenly language and a direct communication with God (1 Cor. 14:2). Human languages are but flesh and that which is flesh is flesh but that which is of the Spirit is spirit.

Taking the Limits Off

Another reason that the Father wants us to pray in tongues is because it takes the limits off Him. He cannot do what He wants to do for us if we do not yield to the Spirit and pray in tongues. Praying in the understanding puts severe restrictions on Him. We must limit God in nothing. We must not only not limit Him in our prayers but He requires our full expression of faith, trust, obedience, patience, love and any of that which is required of His people.

PSALM 78:41 – *Yes, again and again they tempted God, and limited the Holy One of Israel.*

Praying only with our understanding restricts the Father to the finite scope of our human minds. Our decisions on what to pray for, and praying for these things according to our meagre knowledge, puts extreme limits on Him. Furthermore, most of the time our asking for things in our own understanding will not even be in the Father's will. Such kinds of prayers are in most instances actually instructions to God on how we think things ought to be.

I pray that the Father will give you sharp insight into the scripture given below because then you will see clearly how praying with the understanding falls far short of what God could do in the life of the believer. You will also see how the super-abundant ability of God only comes into manifestation in direct proportion to praying at length in tongues. It's all in there.

EPHESIANS 3:20 – *Now to Him who is able to do exceedingly abundantly above all that we ask or think, according to the power that works in us.*

The word 'ask' in the scripture above means prayers that originate out of the human mind and as such can only be for selfish needs (Wuest on Eph. 3:20). When I first discovered this, I was disgusted, as this is a pitiful, beggarly type of praying. This certainly characterizes most prayers in the understanding. This kind of praying amounts to nothing. Even prayers in the understanding that seem to be righteous will always come far short of the glory of God. The effect of praying for things with selfish motives must not be taken lightly. It can be devastating. Settle it in your mind that this is not the way to go.

What is exciting is the praying that is 'according to the power that works in us'. This kind of praying far exceeds our natural prayers. The words 'exceedingly abundantly' refer to outcomes that are in the superlative of superlatives. This kind of praying has to be tongues because praying in tongues is the only type of prayer that is of such a high quality as to bring answers on this level into manifestation.

There is also sufficient revelation in the words 'according to the power that works in us' that points in this direction. The word 'power' is translated into English from the Greek word *dunamis* and this word always refers to the dynamic power of the Spirit of God. The word 'works' is translated from the Greek word *energeo* and means 'the generated energy of the Spirit of God'. When you got baptized in the Holy Spirit, you spoke in tongues and you received this dunamis. After that, if you yield to the Holy Spirit by praying at length in tongues, you will generate the energy of the Holy Spirit. This brings the miraculous into manifestation as it did in the early church and throughout the gospel age. Dunamis, energeo and tongues go together.

We must of necessity pray in tongues because these are the only prayers that are in the perfect will of God. They are the very expressions of the high thoughts of God (Is. 55:8-9), given in words that come directly from the Holy Spirit and are therefore untainted by human thought. This kind of praying takes the limits off God because He can then act on behalf of His children, according to His own omniscient, omnipotent, omnipresent and eternal abilities.

The phrase 'according to the power that works in us' has further revelation. Although praying in tongues takes us out of the limiting prayer of the understanding, we can still limit God by the degree that we yield to the Holy Spirit. The super-duper abundant provisions of God are only released from the throne of God in direct proportion to our praying at length in tongues.

George Jr, our youngest son, is filled with the Holy Spirit and prays in tongues. He believes that by following this path limits on his future will be removed. Like all our children, he emulates the model of operating in the Spirit that we set before him. He holds a firm conviction that he will see a glorious future if he follows hard after this way of life. It's actually a joy to see his keen understanding of the scriptures and his rapid forward movement in the Lord as a result of his praying in tongues.

Time

Time lost in our lives must be redeemed and the Father is urgent. There are many challenges and curved balls that life throws at believers and they are subject to years of subtractions and divisions. The devil and his demons work hard to block the progress of God's plan and purpose for our lives. Behind many people lie years of devastation. For many it seems as though there is no hope. However, God, Who is not in the business of quenching smoking flaxes or breaking bruised reeds (Matt. 12:20), wants to bring rapid deliverance. To deal with setbacks in our lives and to redeem the time, He needs us to dedicate ourselves to praying at length in tongues and to obey Him in all things.

The Word instructs us to redeem the time. This means that we must buy back the time. However, in our own strength and power this is an impossible task. How then shall we redeem the time? You must agree that our only hope of doing this is through the might and power of the Holy Spirit (Zech. 4:6). There is nothing impossible with Him.

And how shall it be done through the Spirit? Through tongues, because only tongues can transcend the gulf of impossibility and redeem the time. How else? Only tongues can bring into manifestation that which would otherwise have taken years to accomplish.

EPHESIANS 5:16 – *Redeeming the time, because the days are evil.*

The fact that God promises us a restoration of lost time does not mean that we will have it by a mere confession. It is prevailing prayer in tongues that gets the redeeming of time on the go. Our bold confession makes it a reality in our lives.

JOEL 2:25 – *So I will restore to you the years that the swarming locust has eaten, the crawling locust, the consuming locust, and the chewing locust, My great army which I sent among you.*

Praying in tongues is not a waste of your time. God never wastes people's time. The truth is that much time has been lost in our lives because of us relying on our own abilities and we are the ones who need Him to fast track things for us. To bring this about, the Father has given us the awesome tool of tongues. The Book of Acts gives us a record of how God does this.

God wanted to bring a salvation breakthrough amongst the Gentiles. So, He sent an angel to a Roman centurion named Cornelius. The angel told him to send for Peter, who would tell him words whereby he would be saved.

Meanwhile, God gave a vision to Peter that prepared him to go to Cornelius. At Cornelius' home, Peter preached the gospel and those who heard him believed. While he was still preaching, God poured out His Spirit on the Gentile family. Thus, the Lord brought these Gentiles into the Kingdom of God with extraordinary speed.

There were no long periods of fasting and prayer, knocking on the doors of the Gentiles, asking them permission to share the gospel with them. No! What would have taken maybe twenty years to bring to pass was accomplished within in a few days through the supernatural. An angel, a vision and the pouring out of His Spirit and, boom, they were in (Acts 10:1-48).

There is no doubt in my mind that the whole matter was kick-started by someone praying in tongues, most probably Peter. We are told that, after the appearance of an angel to Cornelius, on the next day Peter went onto the roof to pray and while praying he fell into a trance and saw a vision. Falling into a trance and seeing a vision happens to people who have already built into their lives the holy exercise of praying at length in tongues. When we pray in tongues, it is the same God Who fast-tracks things in our lives.

The Speed of Tongues

Your praying in tongues and praying in the understanding can be compared to a brand-new, top-of-the-range, sixteen piston, turbo-charged sports car and a small, old, battered car.

Praying in the understanding is like the small car struggling up a long, steep incline, and then trying to overtake a long, articulated truck. The driver first of all struggles up the mountain, and then is faced with the slow-moving truck that needs to be overtaken. He or she hesitates to overtake, tries to peek ahead, but then abandons the attempt as too risky.

However, when the top-of-the-range sports car approaches the scene, the driver sees no problem, presses the accelerator, kicking in the car's standby power, shoots by both and disappears into the distance. This is what praying in tongues is like. It releases the awesome stand-by power of the Holy Spirit (John 14:16 Amplified).

In some cities there is what is called 'the car pool lane'. It's a tremendous advantage. I remember when my family and I were driving on a highway in Los Angeles, we were moving slowly in the traffic when we noticed that there was a lane where traffic was moving fast. After realizing that cars with more than one passenger could use this lane, we shifted into that lane. We then shot by the other traffic and shouted with joy.

Praying in tongues takes you out of the heavy traffic of praying in the understanding and puts you into the spiritual car pool lane, which is speaking in tongues. Praying in tongues gives you the advantage (John 16:7).

The Holy Spirit created and set light in motion. In comparison to the speed of the One who created it, it travels at the slow speed of 300 000 kilometres per second. He has to be faster than that which He created. He cannot create a rock that He cannot pick up, and there is no speed that He has set in motion that He cannot exceed.

An example of this is given to us in the Book of Acts. Phillip was in the desert and had just baptized the African eunuch, when he suddenly disappeared. The next trillionth of one percent of a nano-second, having been caught up by the Spirit of God, he was found at Azostus, many miles away (Acts 8:39-40). This was a Holy Spirit translation in incalculable speed. The same One is in the business of speeding things up for us when we pray in tongues.

To fast-track things in your life, get alone with God and pray at length in tongues. Obey the Lord and you will be amazed at how things begin to change in your life in a rapid way.

4 GETTING GOING

Praying at Length in Tongues

If you want to flow in line with the divine order of doing things (which you will learn about later in this book) and break into the realm where great things happen, you will have to be transformed into a person who prays at length in tongues. An occasional spurt and spattering of tongues here and there will not do. You will have to implement daily two-hour sessions of praying in tongues into your prayer life. If you want this, this is how you do it.

First make a quality decision to pray in tongues for two hours every day. This must be your target and you must be determined to stick to it. If you want the triune God to work for you, then two hours it is, and two hours you must do. Don't be intimidated by the thought of two hours and then say to yourself that you cannot do two hours. You can. The Word says that you can because the Lord gives you the ability. Is it not so?

PHILIPPIANS 4:13 – *I can do all things through Christ who strengthens me.*

You may decide to start with fifteen minutes and then to grow it into half an hour and then into an hour and eventually into a two-hour session. You can also go directly for two hours at the outset, as we did, and you will be there. It's best to start with two hours, but if you start with less, persevere until you have reached your target.

Our first two-hour focused praying in tongues was a cold turkey transition from praying mainly in the understanding to lengthy praying in tongues. The two hours were torture to our minds. There was no slow building up to two hours. We did not first conquer fifteen minutes and continue in victory over that amount of time for a while, and then after that work to beat half an hour, an hour, and eventually, after a few weeks or months, reach two hours. We went straight for the two hours. You can do the same.

Next, set a time for your two-hour focused and uninterrupted praying in tongues. Aim for a specific time of the day that you are going to dedicate to this and stick to it. Before starting your first two-hour session of praying in tongues, inform your family of your decision to do so. Ask them not to disturb you for the two hours, even if they see the Lord coming on the clouds. Resolve not to come out of your prayer closet. Even if you hear the sound of the trumpet and the voice of an archangel, leave in the rapture praying!

At the set time, go into your prayer closet, shut the door behind you, switch your cell phone off, close the curtains, throw a blanket and a pillow on the floor for you to kneel on, and then proceed with your plan to pray at length in tongues.

Matthew 6:6 – *But you, when you pray, go into your room, and when you have shut your door, pray to your Father who is in the secret place; and your Father who sees in secret will reward you openly.*

When you are settled, just open up your mouth and begin to pray in tongues. Go ahead and speak words that come easy to you. Walk about and pray like that for a while. If you decide to kneel, do so. Just carry on praying in tongues and don't return to your learned language. After a while you might find that the going is getting tougher. Don't give up. Push on and pray in tongues. Get up and walk if it keeps you going. Lie down on your bed if it helps you. Swing your arms if it keeps you awake. Dance to keep things alive. Lift up holy hands to glorify God as you pray but do not stop praying in tongues, and do not return to your known language.

Your mind will make it very difficult for you and will protest all the way. Remember that you have been operating through your mind for a lifetime, but now you are starting to operate in the Spirit, so your understanding will not be happy at all. Don't yield to it. The devil and his cohorts will also try to stop you from praying in tongues. Don't listen to them because they are liars. They know from past experience that they must not allow you to achieve this objective. The world is dead to anything that relates to the Spirit of God. The television and a host of other things will beckon. Ignore these calls.

Don't get discouraged. In our case the first fifteen minutes took so long but we soldiered on. We completed half an hour and pushed on until we had an hour under the belt. It was all dry bones, but we persevered until we finally completed two hours. At the end of the two hours, the voice of the Lord broke through, giving us words that began to give us new and fresh direction in ministry. So, press on.

As time rolls on, carry on praying in tongues. Pray softly if you want to, or pray louder if it helps you, but just carry on speaking these words that cannot be understood by your mind. No matter what your mind might be saying to you, the truth is that you are speaking to God (1 Cor. 14:2). You will not be wasting your time because God does not waste people's time! Hear me! God does not waste people's time. Glorious things happen and always happen while believers are praying in tongues.

An hour will pass by and finally you will cover two hours. Before stopping, lift up holy hands, lift your face to heaven and praise God in tongues. After this you can shift back into your own language and praise God with words that by now will be bubbling out of your mouth. Praise God. If you have persevered, you will have finished your first two hours and you will be on a roll. You will have activated the Holy Spirit in you, moved the Intercessor who is at the right hand of God to work on your behalf, and the Father to release His blessings into your life.

Don't stop there. Do the same thing the next day and the next and the next. Follow our example. We continued with our two-hour praying in tongues day after day, week after week, month after month and year after year. Eventually it became easy for us and, needless to say, we have seen the glory of God.

When we first began to implement our daily two-hour sessions of praying in tongues, the Lord gave us Psalm 81:13-16. It was an appeal to us to listen to and to obey Him so that He could bless us. All that He promised in this portion of the psalm came to pass.

Read the psalm and, if you have an ear, listen and obey what is clearly revealed in the scriptures and you will have total victory over all the works of darkness and over all the workers of darkness. Pray in tongues for two hours every day and He will lead you into the finest revelations of His Word. Obey the Lord and honey from the Rock that is higher than you will flow into your spirit and you will be totally satisfied. All the good word of God will come to pass, just as the scripture promises (Joshua 21:45). To God be all the glory, now and forever more.

Plug In

Your decision to embark on a life of praying at length in tongues, and then getting your first two-hour session going, was your act of plugging into the mains of heaven. The Holy Spirit is the central Power House of God and, when you plug in, the power of God begins to flow.

ACTS 1:8 – *But you shall receive power when the Holy Spirit has come upon you; and you shall be witnesses to Me in Jerusalem, and in all Judea and Samaria, and to the end of the earth.*

The Holy Spirit's power and its effect in the spirit realm is like the power and effect of electricity in the natural realm. As natural electricity flows through cables to the point of use, so does the power of the Holy Spirit flow through the Spirit-filled believer to those in need. Those who accidentally come into contact with natural raw electrical power will tell you what power is in the cables. Likewise, those who have come into contact with the power of the Holy Spirit have a story to tell.

The English word translated as 'power' in the scripture given above represents the Greek word *dunamis*. This is the explosive power of God that manifests when miracles are performed. When you got baptized in the Holy Spirit, you received this power. You don't have to wish for, desire or pray for it because the power is already in you. The Lord Jesus Christ Himself said so.

LUKE 24:49 – *Behold, I send the Promise of My Father upon you; but tarry in the city of Jerusalem until you are endued with power from on high.*

Now, whenever you pray in tongues, the inherent power of the indwelling Holy Spirit is released into your spirit. If you continue with your two-hour sessions of praying in tongues, and pray more and more in tongues, more and more power will be released into your spirit. Your diligence will result in the power of God building up in your spirit and you will become charged up like a powerful battery. Although you do not feel the power, it will be in you and it will then be available for use in your life and for your supernatural ministry.

This awesome power will be released into your very praying. Like electricity flows into an engine and powers it up, so will the power of the Holy Spirit flow into your prayers and power them up. Holy Spirit-infused prayers make tremendous power available. The Amplified version of the sixteenth verse of James, chapter five, brings this truth out.

Your witnessing, counselling, prophesying, preaching and teaching will be also be filled with the dynamic of heaven. Men and woman will be as grass before a fire when you speak under the unction of the Spirit. The singing of a born-again, Holy Spirit-filled, tongue-talking singer has far greater impact than any secular singer. Musicians who pray in tongues will have this power flowing through them and as they play the anointing will fill the place.

As you, and more and more members of your local church, pray in tongues, so will the corporate anointing of that church increase. I describe this anointing as the crackling power of God because, as the electric power of God manifests, the people sense sparks flying about and enjoy the thrilling excitement.

Demons will tremble at your arrival because of the power that they know is in you. The spiritual bolts of lightning that flow through you will blast them out of your way. When you lay hands on the sick, the Holy Spirit's power will flow into sick bodies and dissipate the sickness and disease. Cancers and tumours dissolve under this power and nobody will be able to tell what happened to them.

Calynn our daughter believes that the lights come on brightly when we pray in tongues. We were leaving a resort one day and suddenly her spirit was lit up and she became aware of a young boy who was in danger. Although all things looked normal to all the many people who were in the car park, the Holy Spirit showed her that the young boy was being subject to human trafficking. She alerted my wife who immediately sprang into action. After a short enquiry it was discovered that it was indeed so. The men were strangers to the boy and would have driven off with him. The devil's plan was thwarted because she had taken time to pray in tongues. Needless to say, the family of the boy remains ever grateful.

A while back the Holy Spirit said, "Tell the people to plug in". We told our local church to do so. We were already plugged in and they wasted no time in plugging into the mains of heaven. Plug in.

Once you plug in, remain plugged in. Why would you pull the plug out and stop the flow of the power of God? If you pull the plug out, all the lights will go out and you will be forced to use candles.

Daily

This is a daily business. Every day you must arrive in His presence and you must complete your two-hour session of praying in tongues. Of course, there will be times of praying in your understanding that will further enrich your experience, but your praying at length in tongues must be there.

PROVERBS 8:34 – *Blessed is the man who listens to me, watching daily at my gates, Waiting at the posts of my doors.*

Follow the example of daily praying that the Lord Jesus Christ demonstrated when He was on the earth; that is, if you are serious about doing business with the Father.

The Lord engaged the Father in prayer every day. It was not a case of just believing that it was necessary. His supernatural ministry depended on His praying in the Holy Spirit and the urgings of the Spirit got Him going very early in the morning (Mark 1:35). This seems to have been an ingrained daily practice because several parts of the divine record tell us of how the Lord would withdraw Himself from the multitudes and go into the wilderness and mountains to pray. Sometimes He would continue in prayer throughout the night (Matt. 14:23; Mark 1:35; Luke 5:16, 6:12). On one occasion, the Lord Jesus Christ took Peter, James and John and went up onto a high mountain to be alone with them. It was His custom to go alone and to pray in places like this, and the Lord must have been in prayer when He was transfigured before them. This was a supernatural manifestation and could only manifest in a person who prayed in the Spirit daily (Matt. 17:2).

Daily prayer is all about working together with the divine order and on the grand scheme of God's plan and purpose for your life. All things work out for the good. A little is released every day. It might be a Word of Wisdom today or a Word of Knowledge tomorrow. The Father works on things past, present and future, crafting His splendid plan for your life and guiding you into His purpose.

At other times, He adds provision or perhaps a victory in some department of your life to propel you further into His will. He warms people's hearts towards you and works on your behalf to build up a set of genuine friends in your life. Some people are added, and some removed.

At times He reveals self to self, so that you can change for the better. There are many, many little components to God's plan and purpose for your life, and these must be set in place so that you may come into the final victory that He has for you. Daily praying in tongues does it.

LAMENTATIONS 3:22-23 – *Through the Lord's mercies we are not consumed, because His compassions fail not. They are new every morning; Great is Your faithfulness.*

The Father is always mindful of His plan and purpose for our lives. He is forever bursting forth with desire, wanting to release all that we need for the day and for the progress of His plan and purpose. Jeremiah simply calls these things 'mercies' and says that they are 'new every morning'. I combine the thought and call them *new mercies*. If you neglect to engage the divine order on a particular day, you will miss out on the new mercies that were due to you for that day.

The Father will never condemn you for not coming into His presence every day. However, you will lose out on what could have been yours for the day. Although initially a comforting thought, it soon becomes disconcerting.

Yielding

Learn to yield to the Spirit of God. Once you are plugged in, you must get the current of tongues going. This will happen as you yield to the Holy Spirit. You, and not the Holy Spirit, are responsible for the flow. It is your decision, as the scripture below clearly teaches.

---

1 CORINTHIANS 14:15 – *What is the conclusion then? I will pray with the spirit, and I will also pray with the understanding. I will sing with the spirit, and I will also sing with the understanding.*

When you are alone, decide to yield to the Holy Spirit by praying in tongues. To start, open your mouth and speak that which comes easily to you. The Holy Spirit is in you, so be conscious that He is supplying the words. Go ahead and form words by moving your mouth. Try to speak faster and more words will be given to you. It will seem like you are pushing the words out of your mouth. Do this and you will be yielding to the Holy Spirit.

Proficiency and prolific speaking in tongues comes after praying in tongues over a protracted period of time. It takes time before one can get to a position in the Spirit where one can say the same thing as Paul said.

---

1 CORINTHIANS 14:18 – *I thank my God I speak with tongues more than you all.*

At the beginning of your journey in speaking in tongues, you will not be so good at yielding to the Holy Spirit. You might only manage a few words in tongues and then find yourself saying the same words over and over again. Don't be discouraged; this is the beginning, and is not a futile exercise. Carry on and more words will be given to you.

Remember that the unknown tongue, supplied by the Holy Spirit, is a spoken language. It consists of syllables, words, phrases, clauses, pauses, stops and sounds. Some are short words, and some are long words. When speaking in tongues be aware of this and, as you yield, you will find yourself becoming more fluent in your unknown language.

This is how I began. I used to get alone in my room, and then I would just open my mouth and start praying in tongues. I was so interested in this new-found joy that I would listen to myself pray in tongues and would then write these unknown words down. From my writing I could see that I was speaking a clear language.

Continue to yield and one day you will break into a current of tongues. When that happens, don't try to stop it; just give in and speak and the river will continue to flow. At another time you might hit a 'gusher', which is a volume of tongues that surges out of your spirit. Yield to this, and you will find yourself speaking out in more freedom. Continue to yield and at times you will discover that you are speaking in a different tongue. When that happens, chase after it by yielding to the Holy Spirit and speak in the new tongue.

Continue to yield and deeper tongues will be given to you. There will be times when you will find yourself groaning in your spirit, trying to express words that cannot be articulated even in your usual tongues (Rom. 8:26-28). Don't back off from this deep intercession but yield and great things will be accomplished.

When you are alone at work, at home or driving your car, speak in tongues. Don't wait until you feel like speaking in tongues. Don't go by your feelings. Whether you feel like it or not, open your mouth and pray in tongues. My testimony will help you in this direction.

I used to work for an engineering company in 1983 and I was on the management team. My superior apologized profusely when he asked me to spend time sorting out filing in a storeroom. However, I was happy because this task fell in line with my praying in tongues. I would get up early in the morning and pray in tongues and on my way to work I would continue to yield. When I arrived at work, I would rush to the storeroom where I did filing, and when I got there I would just break out in tongues. On most days I would have up to seven hours of undisturbed time praying in tongues as I worked. Words would pour out of my mouth. As I drove home alone, I would pray in tongues. When I got home, I would rush to my room and pray in tongues and sometimes not come out for supper. Needless to say, I became very proficient in speaking in tongues, and the altar calls were filled with souls every Sunday morning.

Follow my exhortation, and there will be a development of the tongue in which you speak and, slowly but surely, you will get more proficient in praying in tongues. You will find yourself speaking in a clear and a definite language.

Yielding has another purpose. The gift of Different Kinds of Tongues must be spiralled into your spirit, like a substance sliding down a curved chute. It is as you yield and pray at length in the Spirit that this will happen.

You are onto a good thing and you must let nothing stop you now. Any progress you make along these lines must be guarded jealously. The Spirit of God encourages you to do so. There are great rewards that lie ahead, and your entire life is going to change now that you are engaging the Spirit of God.

Stir up the Gift

Although you might find yourself praying at length in tongues, the need to stir up the gift will always be there. Of course, there will be times when you will be urged by the Holy Spirit to urgently pray in tongues, but most of the time you will have to stir the gift up yourself. Even after you have learnt how to yield to the Holy Spirit, the need will be there. Paul reminded the young pastor at Ephesus to do so.

---

2 TIMOTHY 1:6 – *Therefore I remind you to stir up the gift of God which is in you through the laying on of my hands.*

You might pray at length in tongues and do great for a while, but then find yourself tapering off and eventually you might stop praying in tongues altogether. Although you know the truth in regard to praying at length in tongues, you might shift away from it and start concentrating on praying in the understanding. The scripture below reminds us all not to neglect the gift that is in us.

---

1 TIMOTHY 4:14 – *Do not neglect the gift that is in you, which was given to you by prophecy with the laying on of the hands of the eldership.*

Tongues will lie dormant in you forever if you do not stir the gift up. The Holy Spirit lives in you, and He is always ready to manifest Himself, but He needs the Spirit-baptized believer to do the stirring up. The responsibility to stir the gift up is on you, and not on the Holy Spirit.

There is a principle that we all must learn. If the Spirit does not move you, you must move the Spirit, and then the Spirit will move you. You start in the natural, and you will end up in the Spirit. You start and the Helper rises up in you. That's how it works.

After Elijah's mantle fell upon Elisha, he made his way back to where the other prophets lived. When he got to the River Jordan, he simply smote the waters with the mantle and said, "Where is the God of Elijah?" (2 Kings 2:14). He did not wait for the Spirit to manifest, but he smote the waters moving the Spirit to act – and He did. The Spirit of God split the river and Elisha crossed over on dry ground.

This principle is easily recognizable in other areas of our flowing with the Spirit of God. Most worship teams will acknowledge that many times, and perhaps most of the time, they hardly feel anointed before Sunday morning worship. However, if they have prepared properly, all that they need do is to start playing their musical instruments and singing and the anointing will show up. They stir up the presence of the Lord, and the anointing begins to flow.

I know that, as a preacher, when I get into the pulpit I must begin preaching or teaching. If I do that, and have prepared in the Word and prayer, the anointing arrives, and we have a blessed message. I begin in the natural, and I end up in the Spirit. The same principle applies to speaking in tongues. Those who do not follow this principle never experience the privilege and joy of the manifestation of the Holy Spirit.

I have found many people who have been baptized in the Holy Spirit, but who only speak in tongues in short spurts. For example, when we stand in a circle with other believers to pray on a particular issue, someone breaks out in tongues as if the Holy Spirit has surprised them. Their bursting out in tongues lasts for perhaps thirty seconds or so. After the rush of tongues subsides, they think that they have expressed spirituality.

People like this must be taught and, if they respond positively to correct teaching, they will build up a structured life of praying at length in tongues. They will have stirred up the gift that was in them and will have been blessed thereafter instead of continually quenching the Spirit of God.

Sensitivity to the Spirit

The Spirit of God will never force anyone to do anything. He knows that only humans have the legal right to operate on the earth. He leads and the believer does. When He wants something to be done, He always prompts, urges and tries to lead the believer in the right direction. After that it becomes the believer's responsibility to yield. If the believer overrules and discards the Spirit's leadings and attends to his or her own agendas, then what the Holy Spirit wanted to do in the believers life will not be accomplished. This refusal to yield to the Holy Spirit is what is meant by the term 'Quenching the Holy Spirit.'

---

1 Thessalonians 5:19 – *Do not quench the Spirit.*

If you pray at length in tongues, you will become sensitive to things of the Spirit. You will find yourself recognizing His prompts, urges and leadings. So when you sense the Holy Spirit leading you to prayer, get alone as soon as possible and start praying in tongues. This leads you into the realm of the Spirit where great things happen. Sometimes it even leads to groanings in the Spirit. This is the deepest level of praying in tongues.

Paul was very sensitive to the leading of the Holy Spirit. An excellent example of this is when the Holy Spirit led him into Macedonia for ministry there. Paul recognized the strong check of the Holy Spirit when he tried to go into Asia to preach the gospel there. That was not the right time for that. God had other immediate plans. When he and his companions tried to go to Bithynia, the halt in his spirit led him to decide against going there. He then followed the leading of the Spirit and went to Macedonia. Paul would have missed the will of God if he were not sensitive to the Spirit. The awesome miracles that followed were as a result of him recognizing how the Spirit was leading.

Acts 16:6-8 – *Now when they had gone through Phrygia and the region of Galatia, they were forbidden by the Holy Spirit to preach the word in Asia. After they had come to Mysia, they tried to go into Bithynia, but the Spirit did not permit them. So, passing by Mysia, they came down to Troas.*

Sensitivity to the Holy Spirit will result in you distinguishing what kind of prayers you are praying when you pray in tongues. Sometimes you might be building yourself up on your most holy faith, at other times you might be engaged in worshipping God and at another time you might be interceding for a believer or travailing for the lost.

An example of sensitivity to the Holy Spirit is when He leads you to pray for the lost. The Spirit begins by prompting and urging you to pray for someone who is unsaved or for an influx of souls. When you get this leading you must separate yourself to be alone with God and yield to Him by praying in tongues. This always leads to praying in tongues for an extended period of time. If you yield to the Spirit like that, the urge develops into a burden that cannot be shaken off and to travailing prayer in the Spirit. Sometimes the burden develops into a kind of spiritual pregnancy for souls. The Spirit builds up the pregnancy until the believer comes up to the time of birth. This takes time and much praying in tongues. When the time of birth arrives, He causes the birth to take place and the lost get born again.

ISAIAH 66:8-9 – *Who has heard such a thing? Who has seen such things? Shall the earth be made to give birth in one day? Or shall a nation be born at once? For as soon as Zion was in labour, She gave birth to her children. Shall I bring to the time of birth, and not cause delivery?" says the Lord. "Shall I Who cause delivery shut up the womb?" says your God.*

If this operation of the Holy Spirit is not followed, the church gets filled with people who have only had an intellectual reception of the knowledge of salvation. For eternal results we must have people born again by the Spirit of God.

If you want to be sensitive to the Spirit's prompts, urges and leadings you must spend much time praying in tongues. When these come you must be willing and obedient to Him and you will eat the fat of the land.

5 THE DIVINE ORDER

Triune God

It is of utmost importance that you understand the divine order of doing things. This is how God works. If you want Him to deal with the devil and his stuff, to pull you out of the doldrums of your life, move you forward in His plan and purpose and work on moving the church forward into greater victory, you must take cognizance of the divine order. God cannot work with ignorance (Hosea 4:6). Life in the kingdom is not a case of, 'God works in mysterious ways, His wonders to perform'.

The divine order of doing things is an open secret, except that God is willing to reveal the workings of it to those who desire to flow with Him. After reading this chapter you will know how the divine order works, and if you flow with God and meditate on this truth you will grow in your knowledge of it. Follow my line of thought and you will be on your way.

First, the scriptures fully persuade me that there is only one God and I confess together with the Jews that there is only one God and that there is no other beside Him (Is. 45:6). There is only one true and living God.

Deuteronomy 6:4 – *Hear, O Israel: The Lord our God, the Lord is one!*

However, I am also fully persuaded that the divine trinity is revealed in many parts of the Law and the Prophets and is fully set forth in the New Testament. The fact that the triune God was not apparent to the Jews of old, and that those who live today are completely blind to it, does not make the teaching of it a false doctrine.

God is One in the substratum of His being, but He manifests Himself in three persons, namely the Father, the Son and the Holy Spirit. The divinity of each and their total unity is clearly taught in the bible. It might boggle the human mind, but it is so. He is the triune God.

---

2 Corinthians 13:14 – *The grace of the Lord Jesus Christ, and the love of God, and the communion of the Holy Spirit be with you all. Amen.*

Below is a brief scriptural layout of how the divine trinity functions. However, if you dig deeper into the scriptures, you will discover beyond any doubt that the Father is the giver, the Son is the Intercessor and the Holy Spirit is the executive arm of the divine will.

The Father Who is the source of all blessings is always poised in heaven, ready to act on our behalf. Every good gift and every perfect gift comes from Him (Jam. 1:17). He gave the Son and He gave the Holy Spirit. He gave the Word and He gave life. The Father is the giver and is indeed the source of all provisions. There are several places in the gospels where the Lord Jesus taught that the Father is the giver (Matt. 7:11; John 16:23-24).

The Son is also positioned in heaven where He functions in His present-day mediatory role in the presence of the Father as our High Priest, (Heb. 8:1) our Advocate (1 John 2:1) and our Intercessor (Heb. 7:25). However, these ministries of the Lord are not automatic. He is ever ready to operate in these ministries but awaits human initiative. We are told that, 'He always lives to make intercession for us'. This must not be erroneously interpreted to mean that He is automatically doing so. The words, 'He always lives', simply mean that He is always alive for the purpose of making intercession. He is always there and always ready.

The Holy Spirit dwells in us and is ever ready to work on the plan and purpose of God for our lives. He is the initiator and the executor of the divine will upon the earth. He always gives substance to all that God does and creates.

Although the Father is ever ready to do and to give, He cannot and will never work independently of the Son and the Holy Spirit. He cannot bypass the Son and the Holy Spirit and work directly with you. Neither can the Son ignore the Father and have something going on with you. The same applies to the Holy Spirit. They always work in perfect tandem with one another and are always perfectly aligned (John 5:30 and 16:13).

Although the angels are not part of the divine trinity, they also play a crucial role in the delivery of the blessings that flow from heaven. So you need to know about them. When the divine order is properly followed and prayer has prevailed, they receive commands from the Father and then work on delivering the answers to prayer. They are ministering spirits sent forth to minister for the heirs of salvation (Ps. 103:21 and Heb. 1:14).

People on the earth also play a critical role in the delivery of what has been reserved for them in heaven. God can do nothing for them without their decision to work with Him. They are free moral agents and have been granted authority and the right to operate on the earth (Gen. 1:26-28). If they refuse or neglect to work with God, then He can do nothing for them.

The Workings of the Divine Order

The Father is a businessperson. The parable of the talents that the Lord told and that is recorded by Matthew pictures Him as a businessperson interacting with His servants (Matt. 25:1-30). The Father is not only a businessperson. He is also a Servant. He Who washed the feet of His disciples said, "He who has seen Me has seen the Father; so how can you say, 'Show us the Father'?" (John 14:9). He is also a Potter because it is written, "But now, O Lord, you are our Father; We are the clay, and You our potter; and all we are the work of Your hand" (Is. 64:8). He also a Vinedresser. The Lord said so and John has the divine record for us: "I am the true vine, and My Father is the Vinedresser" (John 15:1).

As a Servant He serves His people and meets their needs. As the Potter, He moulds and shapes His people, so that they may be more perfect in character. As the Vinedresser, He prunes them, so that they may produce more fruit. As the Businessperson, He works on their prosperity.

DEUTERONOMY 8:18 – *And you shall remember the Lord your God, for it is He who gives you power to get wealth, that He may establish His covenant which He swore to your fathers, as it is this day.*

Now, for the sake of understanding what I am teaching, consider every child of God a legal entity. Each person operates within the system of their country, and has bank accounts, cars, houses, possessions and, to grow his or her life, there is need for food, clothing, shelter and money.

Believers have personal relationships, marriages and careers and all these need to be progressed for the general success of their lives. They have lives to live and, if they surrender all to the Father, they position Him as the Chief Executive of their lives, and He can then guide them into a glorious future.

Some of these believers start companies, and these also have bank accounts and need capital, property, staff, expertise, wisdom and all that goes with it. If the believer totally dedicates the business to God, then the Father becomes the Chief Executive of that business and can help them grow it to total success.

Many have also been called to the ministry, and they have gone out and registered legal entities, such as churches and ministries. These hold bank accounts, properties and various possessions. The head of the church or ministry holds the legal entity on behalf of the Father because they are stewards over His non-profit companies. He is the Chief Executive of each entity, and those in the ministry are His partners.

In each case, the Chief Executive desires to transfer monies, properties and possessions into these entities to add to their wealth. He wants to develop godly people to be used by Him to steer each entity to success. God does all this so that He may establish His covenant upon the earth and bring His people into an abundant life.

What follows is how the divine order works in order to realize the objectives I have briefly described above. This revelation has been such a blessing to us. Picture the heavenly Businessperson in action as depicted below.

Every day the Father steps out as from behind a curtain into His glorious divine office. He is glorious in appearance, dressed in His awesome heavenly garments. He walks regally and purposefully towards His desk. Tucked under His left arm are documents and in His right hand He holds a pen that is studded with diamonds and other precious stones.

When He gets to His desk, which itself is also extraordinary in its palace style carving, He places the documents on its top, and the pen next to them. Both the documents and the pen emanate the glory of God. He then sits down on His huge, kingly swivel chair, spins around rapidly and slows down to a stop. The Chief Executive, shining with glory and bursting forth with desire, is ready to do business with His partners on the earth. The whole heavenly office is filled with the glory of His divine presence.

The Chief Executive then gets up and walks to the windows of His divine office and looks down upon the earth. His eyes scan the whole earth, seeking out those who are ready to engage Him in business.

---

2 CHRONICLES 16:9 – *For the eyes of the Lord run to and fro throughout the whole earth, to show Himself strong on behalf of those whose heart is loyal to Him.*

This is a daily occurrence (Lam. 3:22-23). The glowing documents contain the plans and purposes that the Chief Executive has for every child of God, for every dedicated business and for every church and for every ministry. None of these plans and purposes are set in stone. The heavenly Businessperson desires to write, to rewrite and to upgrade everything that concerns His partners on the earth.

Some of His partners are not found in prayer at all and He can do nothing for them. Others are found only praying in the understanding and He can only work with them on that lowly level. When He finds those who are praying in tongues, He rejoices because He can work with them on the greater supernatural level.

The heavenly Businessperson's partners who are praying in tongues position themselves for a rapid outworking of the divine order. First, the Holy Spirit gives them the perfect prayers to pray in the Spirit for that day. Second, as they push on and pray at length in tongues and prevail, the Son enters His ministry of intercession on their behalf. Third, the Father always receives the intercession of the Son, and His answer is always 'Yes' (2 Cor. 1:20), because the Father always hears the Son (John 11:41-42).

Unfortunately, the Father cannot release any victory, mercy or blessing that is due to His partners if they have any form of unforgiveness in their lives. There are no short cuts. When this has been thoroughly dealt with by them, the Father, now seated at His desk, raises His hand and, with the divine stamp, stamps the document that contains the record of the blessing. He then speaks the word and the blessing rolls out onto the heavenly conveyor belt. The angels, who hearken unto the sound of His voice, go out to work on the delivery of that blessing.

Again, unfortunately for many, although the blessings have been released in the spirit world, and the angels stand ready to minister for the heirs of salvation, they can do nothing if those on the earth do not boldly declare His Word. If and when they do, then the Holy Spirit gives substance to the blessings and makes them a reality and the angels cause the delivery to take place.

When you engage God by praying at length in tongues, and yield to the urges and prompts that He gives you through the Holy Spirit, you start flowing with the divine order of doing things. The divine order includes the Holy Spirit, the Son, the Father, the angels and yourself.

Divine Order in Your Life

Before going to prayer, always make sure that there is no anger, wrath, resentment, un-forgiveness, hatred or bitterness in your life. If you have fallen into this, all your prayers will be put on hold and your bank balance will suffer (Mark 11:24-26). Holiness is crucial when working with the Holy Spirit. You can't indulge in the things of the flesh and be confident that blessings will flow from heaven on your behalf. Prepare yourself before going to prayer.

Once you are ready, separate yourself to be alone with God and then yield to the Holy Spirit by praying in tongues. The Holy Spirit and you will be working together on eternal things, whether you feel like it or not. Continue in a serious, business-like fashion. Don't work with the triune God in a sloppy and casual way. This is serious business that needs a serious approach. You are in session with the Heavenly Chief Executive.

Proceed with your praying in tongues, aiming for your two hours. Don't yield to your feelings or to anything the devil tries to throw at you. You are a spiritual entrepreneur working together with the Heavenly Entrepreneurial Spirit. The Spirit of God is in the business of bringing Spirit-produced blessings into your life. Go ahead and pray at length in tongues, all the while allowing Spirit utterances to flow from your mouth. Know that you know, that you know, that you know, that you know, that you know that the Father and the Son are there, always poised to act in the divine order for your benefit.

At some point in your praying in tongues, you will prevail, and the Son will then enter into His ministry as the intercessor at the right hand of God and the Father will release the blessing if all is clear.

The Provisions of Tongues

God fully provides for every step of His plan and purpose for our lives. He makes provision for the vision and He does this through our praying in tongues.

Your determined prevailing prayer in tongues will result in things happening in your life that will be to people's utter amazement. It will stun those around you and will lift you up to heights that, in the history of your family and peers, have never been attained.

It works like this. When you pray at length in tongues, the Spirit of God, knowing what lies in the future, deals with the journey of your life. Low points are brought up to par and all unnecessary emphasis is brought down. He levels it out. As you continue praying at length in tongues, although you will be totally unaware of what the Spirit is doing for you, He will be straightening out the crooked places and smoothing out the rough patches ahead.

ISAIAH 40:4 – *Every valley shall be exalted, and every mountain and hill brought low the crooked places shall be made straight and the rough places smooth.*

The Spirit of God in His divine weight and power moves over the rough things of your life like a bulldozer moves across uneven terrain and smooths everything out. This is one of the reasons that He needs you to pray at length in tongues. If you stop before prevailing, the work of the heavenly bulldozer stops.

The scripture given below is such a blessing to read. Some people read it and beam at the wonderful promise of God, all the while forgetting that the making of it a reality in their lives will not be by might nor by power but by the Spirit of God. To get the promises of God fulfilled in your life you must pray at length in tongues and if the Spirit gives you this scripture that means He has been working on this. You must then believe it, meditate on it and boldly confess it to make it a reality in your life,

---

Isaiah 45:1-3 – *Thus says the Lord to His anointed, to Cyrus, whose right hand I have held—to subdue nations before him and loose the armour of kings, to open before him the double doors, so that the gates will not be shut: "I will go before you And make the crooked places straight; I will break in pieces the gates of bronze and cut the bars of iron. I will give you the treasures of darkness and hidden riches of secret places, that you may know that I, the Lord, Who call you by your name, am the God of Israel."*

The Lord gave us a word at our initial venture into focused praying in tongues that unpacked promises like the ones given above in very simple terms. He said that when we pray in tongues, "Things become available that were not available before. Money becomes available that was not available before. People become available who were not available before. Cars become available that were not available before. Houses become available that were not available before. Hotel accommodation becomes available that was not available before. Meals become available that were not available before. Favour becomes available that was not available before. They become available for your benefit, for your disposal and for your use. That which would not bend, will bend. That which could never stand, will stand. That which could never move, will move. That which was ever bound, will be loosed. That which was always tightly shut to you, will open up. That which was always tight, will loosen up. Laws will be waived for you. Things that were never allowed before will be allowed. Things that were never done before, will be done for you."

All this gets fulfilled in our lives all the time and brings such joy to us. We pray at length in tongues and, in our journeys, people give us things all the time. Up to now we have never started off with a budget when God has instructed us to go somewhere. We pray in tongues and obey and money that was not available becomes available. Somebody grabs my wife's hand or mine and gives us a 'Pentecostal handshake'. This means they place a thick envelope in our hand, close it and say, "God bless you". Others deposit money in our bank account, that makes it bounce up and down with a loud Kadoomp!

At every city that we arrive in to preach the gospel, there is a person there who is like an angel, helping us achieve our objective. Some act as administrators or as drivers, others as servants who clean and prepare our clothes and others as tour guides who pay for everything. We have lived in mansions, penthouses and luxury resort accommodation that was paid for by others. We have sat in top class restaurants, enjoying fine company and eating meals that, we know, were provided by the Lord.

God's favour has been on us as the morning rising sun. People have said yes, when it was obvious that they wanted to say no. There were situations in our lives that would not bend, that bent. There were departments in our church that were weak, and it seemed that they would not stand, that stood. There were church services which would never move, that started moving again. Finances that were ever bound, were loosened. Doors that were tightly shut, were opened up. Tight relationships were loosened. Laws that should have been applied against us were waived. Things that were never allowed before, were allowed. Things that were never done before, were done for us.

God's provisions were available for our benefit, for our disposal and for our use. Glory to God now and forever more! We travel all over South Africa and to other countries without any money in our pocket to begin with. It is all miraculous.

Spirit-Produced Blessings

All the blessings that originate from God are Spirit produced. They cannot be generated otherwise. This is exactly what the scriptures tell us. Paul made an important statement in this regard.

EPHESIANS 1:3 – *Blessed be the God and Father of our Lord Jesus Christ, who has blessed us with every spiritual blessing in the heavenly places in Christ,*

The word spiritual in the quotation given above does not refer to spiritual blessings as opposed to material blessings, as is erroneously understood, believed and taught by many. The word is a translation of the Greek word *pneumatikos* and this word always refers to the working of the Holy Spirit. An alternate and more accurate translation of the word would be 'Spirit-produced' (Wuest on Eph. 1:3). Paul was actually informing the Ephesians that the Father had blessed them and that these blessings had been made a reality in their lives by the Spirit of God through Christ Jesus. This is how God always worked and still works. The divine ways of doing things are clearly seen in creation and in other things.

GENESIS 1:1-2 AND JOB 33:4 – *In the beginning God created the heavens and the earth. The earth was without form, and void; and darkness was on the face of the deep. And the Spirit of God was hovering over the face of the waters... The Spirit of God has made me, and the breath of the Almighty gives me life.*

The created heavens and the earth and all the things therein are Spirit-produced things. The Father had the plan, the Son spoke it, and the Spirit of God gave substance to it. This truth can also be seen in the salvation experience. The plan of salvation was in the Father's mind, the Son executed it through His work on the cross, and the Spirit produced the born-again experience in us. Creative healing miracles work in the same way. An arm that has been deformed is straightened and made whole through a Holy Spirit-produced miracle (I Cor. 12:11 and Lu. 6:10).

Spirit-produced blessings work like 3D printing. Through this technology, a three-dimensional object is built from a computer-aided design model. A machine, guided by this program, successively adds material, layer upon layer, until the finished product is ready for the next process. Likewise, when one prays at length in tongues, the blessing slowly forms until it is complete and ready to be delivered.

In fact, when you start praying in tongues, the whole of heaven's factory kicks in and begins to operate for your benefit and for His glory. As you proceed, pressing in and prevailing, heaven's machinery picks up speed and produces for you, according to the divine programs in them. I repeat, all of heaven's factory machinery kicks into production when you start praying in tongues.

On our first trip to the USA we made our way down to Orlando, Florida. The Lord helped us, and we ended up accommodated in a lovely resort, very close to the Disney World Parks. However, we did not have sufficient funds to buy tickets to enter the parks. All the way from South Africa to the gates of Disney but no money to go in.

My wife saw how desperate Daniel was to get in, so she encouraged him to exercise his own faith. It was amazing to us. The eleven-year-old prayed for a number of days for several hours in tongues. At that time we were invited to attend a service that was conducted on a Sunday afternoon at about three. All our children were reluctant to go because they had to give up their afternoon swim at the resort pools. We went and were offered seats near the front.

While the pastor was preaching, he came down from behind the pulpit and made his way to Daniel and then proceeded to deliver an accurate prophecy that brought victory for our young son. After the service, the pastor and his family took us to a lovely restaurant and there asked Daniel when his birthday was and what he wanted. Daniel boldly said, "June 23 and I wish I could get into Disney World". The pastor said that it was as good as done, but we would have to come to his Wednesday evening service. He also invited me to preach at that service.

There was no reluctance now. At 7 PM we were seated in the front row. After I preached the pastor made a call for people to give tickets to the missionary family to enter the parks. Sufficient tickets for all of us to enter all the parks were given. Daniel is a man of tongues now.

Back in South Africa, when he was about seventeen years old, he became very interested in sports cars. He desired a muscle car, so he would go into his room and pray about that. One day, after praying for up to seven hours in tongues, combined with fasting, he went into the garage, called his mother and with her present he dragged his hand over where he believed the Mustang would be parked and said, "It's here right now." He followed up his praying with a bold confession of the Word. After about nine weeks a Mustang stood exactly where he believed it would.

Praying at length in tongues is crucial to the production of blessings in the spirit. You might not know what you are praying for, but if you follow the urges of the Spirit and continue praying in tongues until you have a note of victory, Spirit-produced blessings will manifest in your life.

Spiritual Entrepreneurs

God is a rewarder of those who diligently seek Him. This can be seen in the life of Abraham who diligently sought God and obeyed Him. God blessed him with abundant wealth (Gen. 24:35). David did the same and God established his kingdom (2 Sam. 5:12). Solomon's wealth came from the hand of God (2 Chron. 9:1-28). A governor of a Roman province sought a bribe from Paul, and we must agree that one only seeks a bribe from someone who has the means to give a bribe (Acts 24:26). It is significant that each of the aforementioned prophets had the Holy Spirit of God operative in their lives.

God does not reserve His rewards for eternity only, but rewards now in this life too. Those who decide to have a working relationship with Him can expect to be rewarded by God as they pursue His will diligently.

HEBREWS 11:6 – *But without faith it is impossible to please Him, for he who comes to God must believe that He is, and that He is a rewarder of those who diligently seek Him.*

If you dwell in the secret place of the Most High, pray at length in the spirit and obey the Lord, you will prosper in material things. That is a certainty. The Spirit of God produces blessings. All things work out for the good for those who pray at length in tongues. This 'all things work out for the good' includes material things and, with an abundant God, much of that.

The Spirit of God is an entrepreneurial spirit. Those who pray in tongues join in and become spiritual and natural entrepreneurs together with Him. This is how the Holy Spirit does it. When you pray in tongues, He reveals new ideas and new concepts to you by an inward voice, impression or perhaps a vision. At the right time, He will cause the necessary provisions to come into your life, so that you can embark on making things a reality in the physical world. God gives the concept to you, He provides, you do, and you prosper beyond measure.

Praying in tongues is also like doing shopping on the internet. All the words that you speak in tongues are like your fingers touching the keypad of your computer when you do online buying. As you pray in tongues, you touch all the right buttons, and this results in the delivery of God's blessings to you.

Tongues is the way that God is transferring the wealth of the sinner into the hands of the just at this time. As you pray at length in tongues, you will move into a space where the unbeliever will need your services and will pay for them. God will use other miraculous ways to bring this wealth into your possession.

Proverbs 13:22 – *A good man leaves an inheritance to his children's children, but the wealth of the sinner is stored up for the righteous.*

Through the foolishness of tongues, the Lord will confound those who hold the economics of the world in their hands. When they wake up, the economies will be in the hands of the just. We are in this space now. All is for the establishment of His Kingdom and for His glory.

Progress by the Spirit

If you pray at length in the Spirit over a protracted period of time, you will discover that the general progress of your life has moved forward. The Spirit moves you ahead and you will never return to the lower quality of life that you lived before. It's wonderful.

The capacity of your budget increases. You will find that you can afford things that you could not afford before. You will enjoy restaurants that were unaffordable before. You will embark on travels that seemed impossible before. Things begin to improve, all for your joy and for His glory. Eventually you will be established in a fully stable life and money will not be a problem anymore.

When we first started out praying at length in tongues, we had a very unstable congregation. We struggled along with about sixty people. People came and people left. It was a story of continual fluctuation. However, shortly after our new life of extended and focused praying in tongues, the congregation stabilized at sixty, never to drop below that number again. It went up to eighty and never slid back again. We continued to pray in tongues, and we went up to one hundred and twenty never, I emphasize, to go back to eighty again. We went up and stabilized at different numbers until we are now more than five hundred with a promise of three thousand and a huge, exceedingly beautiful facility for the glory of God the Father.

The Spirit progresses us into the prophetic promises that the Father has given us. We will eventually say, "Not a word failed of any good thing which the Lord had spoken to us. All came to pass" (Jos. 21:45).

Open Doors

In our journey in life we need doors to be opened for us. These cannot be opened by our own might or our own power. Some people force situations to suit their agenda and claim that the Lord has opened that door for them. Effectual doors of opportunity can only be opened by the Lord through the power of the Spirit of God (Rev. 3:8; Col. 4:2-4). Paul was aware of this because he said that the door was opened for him.

I Corinthians 16:8-9 – *But I will tarry at Ephesus until Pentecost. For a great door and effectual is opened unto me, and there are many adversaries.*

Spiritual doors of opportunity are like the super security doors that will only swing open with the correct input of intricate passwords and body, voice and facial recognition systems. It is actually awesome to observe how impenetrable fortresses become accessible as the heavy doors swing open when the correct access information has been keyed in and processed.

If you pray at length in the Spirit and if you are faithful over a protracted period of time, you will finally click in the right combination and a door of opportunity will be opened. All that will be left for you to do will be for you to step in by faith. If God opened the door for you, what does it matter if someone says, even in anger and determination, "I will see to it that this door is shut to you".

REVELATION 3:8 – *I know your works. See, I have set before you an open door, and no one can shut it; for you have a little strength, have kept My word, and have not denied My name.*

My wife and I visited a prison in South Carolina in the USA. About forty prisoners who had accepted Christ as their Saviour had gathered to hear the Word of God. I made sure that all had accepted the Lord as Saviour and then guided them to receive the baptism in the Holy Spirit. After that I taught them how to pray in tongues. In my teaching I also taught them that only God could set them free. If they had sincerely repented and prevailed in tongues, God would influence the authorities and the prison doors would be opened for them. Only God could do it.

Job 12:14 – *If He breaks a thing down, it cannot be rebuilt; If He imprisons a man, there can be no release.*

When we returned a year later, about seventy-five percent of them had been released. We rejoiced and then taught the same message that we had taught the year before. God opens prison doors for those who are truly His. Peter, Paul and Silas can testify to that.

A Helpmeet

In 1984 I went away for three days of fasting and prayer. I was single in those days and prayed about my future. I spent most of the three days praying in tongues. On the Saturday morning, after packing up, I took a short walk around the swimming pool. As I stood there looking around the garden, these words floated up in my spirit: "You have need of patience and after you have done the will of God you will receive the promise".

On my way home I continued to pray in tongues and at a certain spot on the highway I broke out into unexpected laughter in the Spirit. I knew that I had victory and drove home full of assurance that the Lord had heard my petition. When I got into the safety of my prayer closet I consecrated myself wholly to God. As the years went by I served God in spirit and truth. The Lord gave me special grace to treat the older women as mothers and the younger ones as sisters.

In 1996 I attended to some business in a city about eight hours drive from Johannesburg. As I drove out of that city I began to pray in tongues and did so all the way home. As I neared Johannesburg I heard these words pop out of my mouth, "I brought you out to bring you in". I wondered what that meant. When I reached home, as I opened the garage door to park the car for the night, the Lord spoke to me in a still small voice saying, "I am going to change your life in a way that you could never change it". In those words I understood that the Lord was saying that He would soon be sending someone to be my wife.

The next day I spent some time working in the garden. While I was busy a feeling came upon me that I can only equate to that felt by Adam when he walked alone in the garden and realized that there was no helpmeet comparable to him. I quickly slipped into the house and prayed softly, "Lord, Your will be done".

Three weeks later a group called REAL came singing in our church. One of the songs that they sang was 'Waiting expectantly for something from the Hand of the Lord'. Ruth was the one on the left and after the end of the concert I went to her and thanked her and she thanked me and I thanked her and she thanked me and we have been thanking one another ever since.

A remarkable romance unfolded. One evening, while driving home from visiting my sweetheart, I passed by the spot that I had laughed in the Spirit so many years before. As I drove by, suddenly, without any thought about what had happened there twelve years before, laughter again bubbled up in my spirit. I released it and was filled with joy. There was no room for any doubt after that. We were married within a year after that experience and went on a glorious honeymoon that was certainly a gift from God. He brought me out of singlehood to bring me into the joys of marriage. Tongues is at the heart of the story.

6 GOD'S PLAN AND PURPOSE

Blessed Final Outcome

God has a perfect plan and a perfect purpose for everyone who has been born into this world. Although some never even enter the first step of His plan and purpose by accepting Christ as their Saviour, this does not mean that He never had one for them. He had and has one for all His creation. The Father is direct and clear about this. He said so in no uncertain terms. The Amplified version of the bible sets this truth out in such a very interesting and revealing way.

JEREMIAH 29:11(AMPLIFIED) – *For I know the thoughts and plans that I have for you, says the Lord, thoughts and plans for welfare and peace and not for evil, to give you hope in your final outcome.*

God said that He had thoughts and plans for the Jews of that day. This is the same as saying that He had plans and purposes for them. It cannot be any clearer. The Father then went on to describe what kind of plans He had for them. He said that these plans were for their welfare and for their peace and that these plans would result in a hope that would lead to a blessed final outcome. This means that God's plans and purposes for them, if followed, would result in them enjoying a successful life in their journey to their final days.

This wonderful promise of God is applicable to all believers. It was not only for the first people who read Jeremiah's prophecy, just as the Book of Psalms was not only for the people in the days of David. The promise is applicable to all believers, then and now.

Unfortunately, some have allowed the devil to speak them out of this glorious promise. They follow a misguided teaching that this promise was only applicable to the Jews of that day. The reason that they have swallowed this false teaching is because they have forgotten that God is no respecter of persons. The truth is that, if God had such awesome thoughts and plans for the disobedient Jews of that day, how much more does He have thoughts and plans for those who are His very own sons?

And what an awesome plan and purpose God has for every one of His children! There is nothing that can compare with it. It will always surpass their most unbridled imaginations and wildest dreams. It includes things that have never ever been owned or experienced in the history of their families. Nobody could ever imagine, have ever seen or ever heard of the glorious things that God has planned for them.

---

1 CORINTHIANS 2:9 – *But as it is written: Eye has not seen, nor ear heard, nor have entered into the heart of man, the things which God has prepared for those who love Him.*

Think about it. God's plan and purpose for every person is so distinct that there is no reference on earth to it. Just as every day is different, and every season is unique, so is there a 'one of its kind' plan for everyone. Just as every created thing has its own individuality, so is God's will for each person. Even as there is a perfect difference in all species, so does His plan for every human being differ from all others.

God's plan and purpose for each individual is not like any that ever existed before, exists at present or will ever exist in the future. His plan and purpose for every person is as unique as their very own finger print.

God is a perfect God. So, it must follow that He only has Plan A for each person. There can never be a Plan B that is hidden up His sleeve. He can never be interested in any other plan that they might have designed for themselves. God wants to bring Plan A, and only Plan A, to pass. How can a perfect God work on an imperfect plan?

Although God has these wonderful plans and purposes for His children, they are hidden in His mind. Notice that, in the scripture given above, God said, "I know the thoughts and plans that I have for you". This means that He alone knows His plans and purposes for you. Nobody could ever know them in their own abilities. Fortunately for all believers, the Holy Spirit knows what these plans and purposes are, and He lives in every one of them.

It is important to point out that the will of God, and the plan and purpose of God, are synonymous terms. Equally important is to know that there is the permissive will of God and there is the perfect will of God (Rom. 12:2). Those who are in the perfect will of God are in the most blessed space that they can be.

The permissive will of God is not the best place to be. God can work with His people on that level, but the devil has some degree of access to them. Those who are out of the will of God are not pleasing to Him. He can do very little for them as they position themselves as open targets for the fiery darts of the pernicious one. Before a life of praying at length in tongues, all believers are in the permissive will of God. Nobody starts off in the perfect will of God.

The Father describes His plans and purposes as His thoughts and His ways through the prophet Isaiah (Is. 55:8-9). He says that in comparison to our plans and purposes that we might design for ourselves, His are as high as the heavens are above the earth. Wow! Those are nice plans. He does not stop there but says that once He reveals them and speaks them, they will come to pass, accomplishing all that He intended for them to do (Is. 55:10-11).

He goes on and says that those who obey Him will eventually come to the place where they will go out with joy and be led forth with peace. People of great stature and those of low estate will break forth into singing at their coming, and all the people will applaud them. Instead of a life of pain and loss, they will have a life of prosperity. The Lord will be glorified, and their testimony will abide forever (Is. 55:12-13). Glory to God, not only now, but forever more!

God's Plan for My Family and Me

When I started out in the ministry, I started out with a bang. The numbers in the church increased rapidly and there was great revival. There were many long hours of praying in tongues, and I knew that there was a great future for my ministry. Deep down inside, I knew the ministry was national and international. However, there came a time when I was just plodding along. Although I did engage in an annual session of praying and seeking the will of God for my life, it became almost a case of marking time. After a while, I thought that I should just build up our church, make some sort of impact in our community and accept preaching engagements as they came. Eventually circumstances made me think that maybe I was just a mediocre pastor after all.

I had no idea at all of the awesome things that God had in store for my family. The manner in which God would supply our every need and the spiritual growth that He had planned for our future ministry was unknown to me. I had no inkling of the miraculous transformation of our community that God had in mind. That we were to help so many churches in South Africa and preach the length and breadth of the United States of America was a secret that God was yet to reveal.

Revealing the Future

The Holy Spirit dwells in you and wants to show you things that relate to your future. The Lord said that this was part of what the Holy Spirit, Who is the Spirit of Truth, would do when He came.

JOHN 16:13 – *".... and He will tell you things to come."*

Once more I must remind you that, although this promise was given to us, it does not become a reality in our lives just because it is recorded in the bible. There is something we must do to bring the promise to bear in our lives. We activate the Spirit by praying in tongues. In our sessions of praying at length in tongues, the Spirit of God shows us things that the Father plans to bring to pass in our lives. He does this by the Word of Wisdom. This gift is properly defined as 'a manifestation of the Spirit of God whereby God's plan and purpose for the future is revealed'. The Father reveals the future by an inward witness, an audible voice, a vision, a dream, a visitation of an angel or even a direct appearance of the Lord Jesus Christ Himself.

In our case the Holy Spirit showed my wife and me what would befall us in the future. Out of the blue, He revealed to us that we were to go to the United States of America for six months. This came to pass. While we were there, He revealed to us where to go to. When we got back to South Africa, He showed us that we were to go back a second time and then a third time. By visions and dreams He revealed to us our purpose there. He also showed us the direction of our ministry in South Africa and the many details concerning it.

Many of the things He has shown us have come to pass and many more are yet to break forth. One thing I know is that the final outcome of our lives will be exceedingly blessed. I have no fear or insecurity concerning the future knowing all the good words spoken by the Lord will come to pass in their season.

It's a tricky one though. The things that God speaks are too vast for our finite minds. We often wonder how the Lord will join all the seemingly unconnected things in the future into a perfect fabric. It is all impossible for us to bring to pass. It is too big and too wonderful for us.

It is tricky because the human thought springs immediately into thinking that what God said will come to pass soon. However, we have learned that it all requires faith, trust, obedience and patience because only God can bring to pass that which He has said. If we attempt to bring it to pass, even thinking what we are doing is in obedience to His will, we fall flat on our faces. There is a perfect timing in the mind of God, and we must allow Him to command us and allow Him to do His thing.

His Plan for You

In your very first two-hour session of praying at length in tongues, God will have started working on His divine plan and purpose for your life. The triune God never delays on the matter. He has a perfect plan and a perfect purpose for you and starts working on that immediately.

Your focused praying at length in tongues builds a strong witness in you on what direction to take in life. This involves being led by the Spirit.

There are several things that you need to do in order to have the Spirit lead you. You must combine your praying at length in tongues with a consecrated life. Refuse to follow what you want in life, deny your own desires, wants and selfish ambitions, and do not try to implement your own plans and purposes. With God, never be like Israel of old who insisted they wanted a king to rule over them instead of a prophet like Samuel. That was not God's perfect plan for them at that time and they paid the price for insisting on their own will (1 Sam. 8:1-22).

Follow the inner witness that is given to you by the Holy Spirit and God will guide you into His perfect plan and purpose for your life.

The Lord adds to the inner witness as you continue in your sessions of praying in tongues. The Spirit will give you a little here and a little there. Revelation of His plan and purpose might come to you in the form of a dream, a word of wisdom, a specific leading and maybe through a vision. All this will contribute to the slow revealing of His plan and purpose that God has for you. The full plan will not come all at once. If that were to happen, then there would be no need for faith, for trust, for obedience or for patience from your side. God will only reveal more of His plan to you as you step forth in obedience, following His leading.

Your praying in tongues will allow the Spirit of God to work on getting you out of the permissive will into the perfect will of God. One revelation of His plan will lead to more prayer and more intercession. As He reveals part of His plan for you, then you will be able to pray in the understanding about that.

In addition to praying at length in tongues, you must follow hard after the Lord by walking in faith, by trusting that all is working out according to what He said, by giving Him explicit obedience, by being patient while His plan and purpose is coming to pass and by praying in the Spirit and in the understanding.

The final outcome of your life, if you continue pursuing God's plan and purpose for your life, will be like the opening night of a great Holy Spirit-inspired convention. On this night, all the different components of the preparation for the convention kick in. The music starts and the explosion begins. The people are swept into the glory. The preacher steps out and the anointing comes down. The preaching is with power, the night is a success, and everybody leaves rejoicing.

Every leading, every word of knowledge, every word of wisdom, every vision, every Holy Spirit-given dream, every obedience, every song, every prayer in the understanding and every spiritual progress that has come through praying in tongues, will turn out for your good (Rom. 8:28). It all leads to the explosive moment when you reach the full extent of your life and ministry.

7 DIVINE ILLUMINATION

Insight

Don't be satisfied with a laborious and boring study of the scriptures. As a Spirit-filled believer, you can receive divine illumination of the Word of God. Illumination is when the Holy Spirit gives a Spirit-filled believer divine insight into scripture. These scriptures were initially given by revelation to the prophets of the Old Testament and the apostles of the New. They then captured these revelations in writing under the inspiration of the Holy Spirit.

Nobody can receive new revelations and be inspired to write fresh new scripture after that which was written by the apostles who lived in the days of the Book of Acts. Today, the scriptures get illuminated by an operation of the Holy Spirit. They were Spirit-given and Spirit-inspired and now they are Spirit-illuminated. Mentally understanding the Word cannot be compared with the Holy Spirit-given enlightening of His Word.

You receive illumination of scripture when you dig deep into the scriptures and if you pray at length in tongues. This is proven to be true as we search the scriptures that relate to things of the Spirit of God. Paul wrote to the Corinthians, telling them what happens when they pray in tongues.

---

1 CORINTHIANS 14:2 – *For he who speaks in a tongue does not speak to men but to God, for no one understands him; however, in the spirit he speaks mysteries.*

First, in some cases, when you are praying in tongues, the substance of your praying will be 'mysteries'. This is the word that Paul chose to describe what takes place when we are praying in tongues. It has a very significant meaning and must be clarified if you are to get the full import of what the scripture teaches. The Greek word is *musterion* and means, 'that which is known to the mustes'. The *mustes* were those who had been initiated into the mysteries of the secret societies. They were given knowledge concerning their society that was withheld from those who were uninitiated. Although deceived, they considered themselves to be the enlightened ones (Vine's: mysteries).

Born-again ones are the 'mustes' of God. They have been 'initiated' into the Body of Christ by their baptism in the Holy Spirit. They are sons of God, incognito in this world. They are in this world but not of this world. The revelation of Christ Jesus that is gradually illuminated to them makes them the truly enlightened ones.

The word 'musterion', as used in the scriptures, has absolutely no shade of meaning that could suggest riddles or enigmas, nor of any puzzling things that might be in the believer's life. It refers to the knowledge concerning Christ.

Colossians 1:26-27 – *The mystery which has been hidden from ages
and from generations, but now has been revealed to His saints. To them
God willed to make known what are the riches of the glory of this mystery
among the Gentiles: which is Christ in you, the hope of glory.*

This knowledge was hidden from the human mind throughout the ages
before the first advent of Christ. The wicked, of course, could not know
anything about the coming of the Son of God. The Jews in general
were totally unaware of it. Those who prophesied about it did not have
revelation of what it was all about. Even those who walked closely with
the Lord could not understand the things that He referred to (John
16:12).

After the Holy Spirit was poured out on the Day of Pentecost, God
raised up apostles and through certain of them He revealed this mystery.
Through inspiration given by the Spirit of God, they wrote down these
things (Eph. 3:3-7). Now, although the revelation of Christ was given
to them, and is plainly written in the New Testament, it still needs
divine illumination. Truths of Christ, the New Covenant, the Church,
the divine Trinity and the like, can only be illuminated to us by the
Holy Spirit. These things are outside the range of natural apprehension.
Hence the terms especially associated with the subject are 'revealed',
'made known' and 'manifested'.

Now here is the joy of it all: when you pray in tongues you speak
directly to God about the 'musterion' of Christ. In the first scripture
given above Paul says, "…in the spirit he speaks mysteries". So, this
is what happens many times when you are praying in tongues. The
substance of your talking involves divine secrets (mysteries) relating

to the Kingdom of God. God has positioned you for this awesome privilege. You are the 'mustes' of God. Aren't you overjoyed about that?

There is a working of the Spirit of God (1 Cor. 12:4) called 'the spirit of wisdom and revelation' (Eph. 1:17-18) that you need to know about. When you pray at length in tongues this department of the Spirit gets activated and He enlightens the eyes of your understanding, giving you sharp spiritual insight into the mysteries of Christ. The spiritual knowledge that you gain propels you further into the mysteries of the Kingdom. Those who have not been enlightened know nothing at all of the glory that you have moved into.

Taught early in my spiritual walk with God to pray Paul's prayer that is recorded in the first chapter of Ephesians, and to combine it with extended periods of praying in tongues so that I could develop rapidly in Christ, I embarked upon it. This has been my practice over the years and any advance of mine in the Word is a consequence of this.

What follows are notes on 1 Corinthians 2:6-16 that will give you greater understanding of revelation. Paul was at the high end of maturity in the Spirit when he wrote the words below. Read the entire portion of scripture, consider my notes and allow the Holy Spirit to reveal its full force to you.

However, we speak wisdom among those who are mature, yet not the wisdom of this age, nor of the rulers of this age, who are coming to nothing. But we speak the wisdom of God in a mystery, the hidden wisdom which God ordained before the ages for our glory, which none of the rulers of this age knew; for had they known, they would not have crucified the Lord of glory. # Paul essentially says that there is nothing in all the universities of men that can reveal the mystery of Christ and why God used the foolishness of the crucifixion to bring salvation. He only spoke these things to mature Christians, preaching the simple gospel to the lost.

But as it is written: "Eye has not seen, nor ear heard, nor have entered into the heart of man the things which God has prepared for those who love Him."

Paul, who had been educated at the University of Tarsus, the best in the world at that time, makes it clear that the mystery that provided a certain eternal future did not come from the knowledge of humans. That it never 'entered the heart of man' is important. This means that this mystery never occurred to anyone. He held that no one in all their wildest imagination could ever think up God's wonderful plan of redemption and all that came with it. The mystery of Christ did not originate in the consciousness of man.

But God has revealed them to us through His Spirit. For the Spirit searches all things, yes, the deep things of God. For what man knows the things of a man except the spirit of the man which is in him? Even so no one knows the things of God except the Spirit of God. Now we have received, not the spirit of the world, but the Spirit who is from God, that we might know the things that have been freely given to us by God.

Paul makes it clear that only the Holy Spirit can and could reveal the mystery of redemption to mankind. The 'things' spoken of are the thoughts of God on the matters of Christ. Only the Spirit of God can fathom the depths of the heart of God (Rom. 8:26-28). God initially sent His Spirit to dwell in the hearts of the apostles so that He could reveal these things to them via their born-again spirit. The revelation came from within, independent of the knowledge that is taught in any of the learning institutions of this world.

These things we also speak, not in words which man's wisdom teaches but which the Holy Spirit teaches.

Here is the secret of how this divine revelation came to the spirit of the apostle. Tongues is what did it. The words that 'we also speak' are not words that he learnt by human education, that is, 'not in words which man's wisdom' gives us. Paul could speak Hebrew and Greek. He learned these languages by careful human instruction. However, the 'words which the Holy Spirit gave him' were supernatural utterances that did not originate from and were not understood by his human mind. It is written, "For he who speaks in a tongue does not speak to men but to God, for no one understands him; however, in the spirit he speaks mysteries (1 Cor. 14:2). The musterion is spoken out in tongues.

Comparing spiritual things with spiritual.
The word 'comparing' means, 'to judge with' (Wuest). The word 'spiritual' is 'pneumatikos' (Vine's). This word always refers to the working of the Holy Spirit and never means spiritual as opposed to the physical. A more accurate translation would be Spirit-produced and in this case Spirit-given. 'Spiritual things' can only refer to divine revelation that Paul received because that was the subject that he was dealing with. The second use of the word spiritual must refer to the Old Testament scriptures because Paul was comparing his revelations to something Spirit-given. A paraphrase of the portion of the scripture could therefore be, 'Using the revelation that has been Spirit-given and comparing that with that which already has been given by the Spirit of God.'

Paul says essentially the same thing that Peter said: "Knowing this first, that no prophecy of Scripture is of any private interpretation" (2 Peter 1:20). Paul carefully compared the revelation that he received with the Spirit-given Old Testament scriptures, making sure they matched. Thereafter he could be sure that what he gave the people was in line with what was already written. Unknown to him, in his carefully chosen words under the inspiration of the Holy Spirit, he was leaving an infallible record for posterity.

But the natural man does not receive the things of the Spirit of God, for they are foolishness to him;
\# The word 'natural' is 'psuchikos' and means that which belongs to the soul (Vine's). The 'natural man' refers to the unsaved person who, although highly educated, does not have the Spirit of God and includes believers who are body – and soul-ruled. Paul says that this kind of person rejects things of the Spirit because in his or her opinion they are foolishness. The person applies his or her reason to divine revelation and makes no sense of it at all.

Nor can he know them, because they are spiritually discerned.
\# It is impossible for the natural man to know the things of the Spirit because they are Spirit-given and Spirit-illuminated.

But he who is spiritual judges all things.
\# The word spiritual is 'pneumatikos' with the meaning as explained above and refers to the Spirit-infused and Spirit-controlled believer. The word 'judges' means, 'to examine, investigate, question'. Paul says that it is only the Spirit-infused and Spirit-controlled believer who can rightly compare revelation to scripture.

Yet he himself is rightly judged by no one.
\# The 'pneumatikos' man is dismissed as foolish by the 'psuchikos' man but the 'psuchikos' man has no basis to probe the 'pneumatikos' man because he cannot understand the holy.

For "who has known the mind of the Lord that he may instruct Him?" But we have the mind of Christ.
The natural man does not know the thoughts of God, that they should tell Him how to bring about eternal life or not. The Spirit-controlled believer receives the thoughts of Christ.

All Truth

The Lord Jesus Christ prepared His disciples for the dispensation that would follow His exaltation. The inauguration of the New Covenant was imminent. His disciples had not yet received the Holy Spirit in their lives, and the Lord knew that they would never be able to grasp the truths of His work of salvation until they were baptized in the Holy Spirit. In the scripture given below, He essentially told them that they would only receive divine revelation of these things after they were filled with the Holy Spirit.

JOHN 16:12-15 – *I still have many things to say to you, but you cannot bear them now. However, when He, the Spirit of truth, has come, He will guide you into all truth; for He will not speak on His own authority, but whatever He hears He will speak; and He will tell you things to come. He will glorify Me, for He will take of what is Mine and declare it to you. All things that the Father has are Mine. Therefore I said that He will take of Mine and declare it to you.*

The Spirit-filled believer must pray at length in tongues and this gets the Spirit of Truth operating. As He is activated, He does what the scripture above says. He takes of the truth of Christ and transmits it to the spirit of the believer.

The full truth of the revelation of Christ is resident in the Holy Spirit. He knows all things and He is the omniscient One who can reveal the knowledge of the truth. Spirit-filled believers have an advantage. Their praying at length in tongues makes them keen in knowing the truth and in discerning truth from error.

---

1 JOHN 2:20,27 – *But you have an anointing from the Holy One, and you know all things. ...But the anointing which you have received from Him abides in you, and you do not need that anyone teach you; but as the same anointing teaches you concerning all things, and is true, and is not a lie, and just as it has taught you, you will abide in Him.*

The anointing is in us and the more we pray in tongues the more the inner witness establishes us in the truth that is in us. We can tell when something is not of God. We don't have to run to someone to tell us to avoid error. Christians who pray in tongues can go into any city and tell whether a church is in the truth or not.

8 WATERS OF THE SPIRIT

Rivers of Living Water

If you pray at length in the Spirit, you can expect rivers of living waters to flow out of your spirit into this world. This is a promise that the Lord Jesus Christ Himself made. Every Spirit-filled believer who knows how to yield to the Holy Spirit can enjoy this experience.

JOHN 7:37-38 – *On the last day, that great day of the feast, Jesus stood and cried out, saying, "If anyone thirsts, let him come to Me and drink. He who believes in Me, as the Scripture has said, out of his heart will flow rivers of living water."*

Think about it. Supernatural rivers of living water, that originate directly from the throne of God, flowing through and out of your belly to water the world around you. Isn't that awesome?

Love is a river that can flow out of your spirit into the lives of people in your world and can enrich these relationships. Joy is also a glorious river that will change attitudes around you. You have heard people say,

"Peace like a river," and that is exactly what it is. What a wonderful river.

Long-suffering, kindness, goodness, faithfulness, gentleness and self-control are all marvellous rivers designed to be a blessing to those around you (Gal. 5:22-23). Tongues, interpretation of tongues, prophecy, words of wisdom, words of knowledge, discerning of spirits, gifts of healing, working of miracles and special faith (1 Cor. 12:8-10) are all rivers of living water that bring life to the needy.

When the Lord Jesus Christ said rivers, He meant what He said: not one, but many. Each ministry is a powerful river and so is each anointing, divine strength, wisdom, revelation knowledge, song, musical note and every witty invention. These are but a few of these rivers of living waters that can flow out of your spirit.

Unfortunately, these rivers will not flow out of your belly just because the Lord made the promise or as a consequence of the Spirit dwelling in you or as a result of you confessing it. These springs, that become streams and eventually rivers are locked up in your spirit. It is your responsibility to draw from the wells of salvation and to release these to the world

---

Isaiah 12:3 – *Therefore with joy you will draw water from the wells of salvation.*

When you yield to the Holy Spirit and speak at length in tongues, these rivers are released. The needed, pent up pressure of the Holy Spirit is already in your spirit, and when you pray in tongues you open up the floodgates and the rivers of living waters begin to flow out of your spirit.

Praying in tongues does not always produce a gusher. At times, a simple, quiet leading to obey a particular scripture on love is given. As you obey, the result will be a trickle that will grow into a stream and eventually a huge river of love. The same applies to all the other wonderful rivers of living water. They will water your parched world and eventually your valley will be green.

One of these rivers that I have been privileged to have flowing through me over the years is the teaching anointing. A great many people have drunk from that river and have been established in the knowledge of God. It is a river of living water that continues to flow, even through the writing of this book.

Carry on praying for long stretches of time, and you will cause rivers of living water to flow from your belly. These waters may start as a trickle but will become running waters that will come up to your ankles, then to your knees and then to your waist, until it becomes so deep that you will have to swim in what has become an uncrossable river. These waters will flow into the sea of humanity and will bring healing to them. Dead men walking will be brought back to life. A great multitude of souls will be saved and will fill up the churches of pastors who are in the business of catching fish. All along the banks of the rivers, fruitful lands will spring up that others will benefit from and enjoy (Eze. 47:1-12).

Watering Your World

Rain and snow have a specific purpose. They water the ground so that plants may grow and produce fruit for the dwellers on the earth. This also gives them seed, so that they can plant again to get another harvest.

Isaiah 55:10 – *For as the rain comes down, and the snow from heaven, and do not return there, but water the earth, and make it bring forth and bud, that it may give seed to the sower and bread to the eater.*

The words of God have the same effect that natural rain and snow have upon the earth. They water our spiritual landscape with the purpose of having it produce fruit. This effect is not only caused by our speaking the written word, but also by the words that are spoken in tongues, when we pray these out. Tongues are Spirit words encompassing the high thoughts of God that are verbalized by you. They water your world.

Isaiah 55:11 – *So shall My word be that goes forth from My mouth; It shall not return to Me void, but it shall accomplish what I please, and it shall prosper in the thing for which I sent it.*

Pray in tongues and, even if your valley is as dry as an old bone and you are in the worst drought of your life, things will change for the better. Your sunburnt grass, your dry, drooping trees and your scorched landscape that has been devastated by the sun of life will be watered and soon your whole valley will be green, lush and filled with all the fruits of life. This is what tongues does.

The land of milk and honey that Moses spoke of was the land of Canaan that lay beyond the Jordan. It was a good land that was filled with brooks, fountains and springs that flowed out of the valleys and hills. The harvest there was an abundant produce of wheat and barley, grapes, figs, olives and honey. It was a land where bread was eaten without scarcity and where there was no lack (Deut. 8:7-9).

The natural land of Canaan that Moses spoke of was also prophetically the Kingdom of God. This Kingdom is not meat and drink but righteousness, peace and joy in the Holy Spirit (Rom. 14:17). As the physical Canaan was, so the spiritual one is. It is a land of abundance (John 10:10).

Again, unfortunately, the above is not made a reality by just the fact that it is promised and by believers simply confessing it. It is prevailing prayer in tongues, and a confession that follows, that brings it into reality. The brooks, fountains, springs and rivers begin to flow when the believer embarks on a life of praying in tongues. All the blessings of God are Spirit-produced, and when victory is gained a bold confession must follow.

We are all invited to enter into a land of milk and honey and the entire prophecy given in the eleventh chapter of Deuteronomy is given because it is such a blessing to those who want to possess the Kingdom of God.

DEUTERONOMY 11:9-15 – *And that you may prolong your days in the land which the Lord swore to give your fathers, to them and their descendants, 'a land flowing with milk and honey.' For the land which you go to possess, is not like the land of Egypt from which you have come, where you sowed your seed and watered it by foot, as a vegetable garden; but the land which you cross over to possess is a land of hills and valleys, which drinks water from the rain of heaven, a land for which the Lord your God cares; the eyes of the Lord your God are always on it, from the beginning of the year to the very end of the year. 'And it shall be that if you earnestly obey My commandments which I command you today, to love the Lord your God and serve Him with all your heart and with all your soul, then I will give you the rain for your land in its season, the early rain and the latter rain, that you may gather in your grain, your new wine, and your oil. And I will send grass in your fields for your livestock, that you may eat and be filled.'*

This land that flows with milk and honey that we go into to possess, needs no human effort to cause it to produce. Tongues gets the job done. We do not water it 'by foot'. Tongues gets the job done. The Kingdom of God is not a vegetable garden but huge farms. It is not by might, nor by power, but by the Holy Spirit.

It does not matter how bad your situation is now, if you begin and continue with a life of concerted praying in tongues, God will open rivers in the desolate heights of your life and will cause fountains to break forth in the midst of your valleys. He will make your wilderness a pool of water. Your dry, parched and cracked land will become springs of water. All that is yours will flourish again (Is. 41:18-19 and 43:19-20).

Refreshing

Christians, at times, get themselves into a spiritual rut. They start off on fire for God and serve Him with joy and enthusiasm, but in the process of time their service tapers off. They then enter into a phase where they get into repetitive service. These believers find themselves doing the same things over and over again, fulfilling their duties in the church as an obligation. Zest for serving the Lord gets lost. The answer to this problem is found in the scripture given below. Although, this scripture makes reference to the salvation of unbelievers, the principle also applies to the believer.

ACTS 3:19 – *Repent therefore and be converted, that your sins may be blotted out, so that times of refreshing may come from the presence of the Lord.*

Where believers pray at length in tongues, the Holy Spirit has free sway and He can do what He wants to do. The Spirit always desires to refresh believers who get themselves into a dry patch, so that they may become productive in the kingdom of God again. Allowed to move, and having qualities like water, He rejuvenates and refreshes the born-again spirits of the believers. When the Spirit moves like this, believers must recognize this and must make quick adjustments. Those who have fallen into critical thoughts, anger, bitterness, hatred and various other sins must turn away from these. This must be done on the spot. The cleansing blood of Jesus will flow, and the refreshing of the Holy Spirit will break through. This will bring a whole new liberty of spirit for these believers and they will once more immerse themselves in the glorious work of the Lord. It's wonderful.

This can at times happen in the private lives of believers who have been baptized in the Holy Spirit. They find the Holy Spirit dealing with them, they get alone with Him and there they break down. They turn away from what is displeasing to God and the Spirit refreshes them.

This is how spiritual health and a fresh anointing is maintained. The believer must pray at length in tongues, pray in the understanding, remaining in thanksgiving, praise, worship and in sweet obedience to the Word of God. Just as natural health and freshness is visible for all to see, so is spiritual health and freshness.

PSALM 92:10 – *But my horn You have exalted like a wild ox; I have been anointed with fresh oil.*

As a pastor, I observed how believers who had been on fire for God lost their position in the Spirit. They got involved in family squabbles, church politics, business demands and allowed other things to creep in and they became disillusioned. Others lost confidence and faith in the promises of God. The need for counselling became imminent.

However, before I could counsel, the Spirit of God moved in our services and broke down hard hearts. Christians turned from their sins and a refreshing from the Spirit of God flowed in our midst. I stood amazed as these same believers rose up with new vim and vigour and began serving the Lord in spirit and truth. Great and mighty is the Spirit of God.

9 BUILDING UP YOUR SPIRIT

Rest

Praying in tongues is a means of bringing rest to the weary spirit of the believer. A passage of scripture in the twenty-eighth chapter of the Book of Isaiah is identified by Paul as a reference to tongues. In it we have this clear promise made by the Lord to the Spirit-filled believer.

ISAIAH 28:11-12 – *For with stammering lips and another tongue He will speak to this people, To whom He said, "This is the rest with which You may cause the weary to rest," and "This is the refreshing"; Yet they would not hear.*

The human spirit gets tired, just as the human body gets tired. If you labour in spiritual things, such as praying, preaching, counselling, dealing with the devil and the like, your spirit will get tired. If nothing is done to rectify the situation and you continue to engage in extensive spiritual work, your spirit will get exhausted and you will find it very difficult to continue with spiritual work. This can be called a spiritual burnout.

Do not underestimate the effect of spiritual output. Witnessing to an unbeliever will draw spiritual power out of you because the devil tries to hold onto the unbeliever. Your prayers, rebuking him and speaking under the anointing, all constitute a spiritual battle for that soul. The result is that your spirit gets tired. Spiritual counselling has the same effect. The natural delivery of a motivational speaker cannot be compared with the preaching and teaching that is done under the power of the Holy Spirit. When he or she is in the pulpit, the anointed preacher is faced with a mass of thoughts, opinions, beliefs, traditions and determined opposition of demonic forces. All of this drains and tires the spirit. Ministering healing, casting out demons and intercessions are pure spiritual work and have an effect on the spirit of the believer.

This spiritual tiredness is not the burnout that is caused through excessive and prolonged work on the job, projects, business or administrative work. This burnout brings a person to the point where they cannot continue productively. People who do not attend to this kind of burnout become cynical, and feel hopeless, helpless and resentful.

Spiritual burnout is completely different. It leaves one having no power to pray, to witness, to preach or to teach the Word of God. The believer finds himself or herself unable to swing the Sword of the Spirit. Strength to run the spiritual race that is before them is lost. You must not leave things as they are because things will not change unless you rectify the situation. You need to wait upon the Lord.

Isaiah 40:31 – *But those who wait on the Lord shall renew their strength; They shall mount up with wings like eagles, they shall run and not be weary, they shall walk and not faint.*

The way to deal with spiritual burnout is to get alone with God and use the majority of your time there, praying softly in tongues. During that time, don't engage yourself in any kind of spiritual work at all. There must be no praying for the lost, preaching, teaching or casting out of demons while you wait upon the Lord. Just lie on a bed and whisper softly in tongues. Do that for perhaps an hour and focus on getting the mind and body quiet. Rest your body and then pray again in the spirit for a while. Do it again. Combine this with fasting, and all the while you will be resting and refreshing your spirit.

Just as your body relaxes when you rest, resulting in new vigour and vitality when you rise up, so will your spirit be invigorated and revitalized when you follow the plan above. Slowly but surely you will overcome your spiritual faintness and tiredness and be ready to run the race again. In your time of waiting upon the Lord, a new freshness will ooze from the Holy Spirit into your spirit.

Strengthening

God's strength is unlimited. This strength is inherent in the Holy Spirit by virtue of His divine nature. He is the Strengthener. If you spend time praying at length in tongues, He will strengthen your inner man with the miracle power of God.

EPHESIANS 3:16 – *that He would grant you, according to the riches of His glory, to be strengthened with might through His Spirit in the inner man,*

Praying in tongues gives more divine strength to the believer. It's a reinforcement from heaven. When the believer prays at length in tongues the strength of the Spirit of God is poured into the spirit of the believer. No demonic onslaught can move and prevail over the person who has chosen this path.

Renewing

Praying in tongues renews the inward man. It is our responsibility to pray in tongues every day because the inward man is renewed day by day. Just as the outward man has been set on a path of progressive decay by the principle of death, so the inward man has been set on a path of progressive renewal by the principle of life that dwells within. We increase or delay the progressive decay of our bodies by our lifestyle, eating habits and the like. We also progress the renewal of our spirit by our activating the Spirit of God in us. This is done by praying at length in tongues. How else?

---

2 CORINTHIANS 4:16 – *Therefore we do not lose heart. Even though our outward man is perishing, yet the inward man is being renewed day by day.*

The bible is clear that the spirit of man has been born again (1 Peter 1:23; Titus 3:5). The spirit is described as having been regenerated. This initial operation of the Holy Spirit continues, although it should not to be thought of as a fresh giving of the Spirit every day. As the Spirit-filled believer prays at length in tongues, so does the indwelling Spirit progress the development of the born-again spirit of the believer every day.

There must be a progressive development of the new man that lives within. The believer cannot sit by and hope it will happen. He or she must co-operate with the Spirit of God. This is done by daily praying in tongues. This gradually progresses the new man into the image of Christ, assisting it to operate in the Kingdom of God that it has been graciously ushered into.

Edification

The Spirit of the believer needs to be edified. This is accomplished by your praying in tongues, and by your assimilation of the Word of God into your inner man and your practising it. A combination of both are essential for balanced spiritual development.

The building up of the born-again spirit that is achieved by speaking in tongues is clearly taught in the epistles. Two scriptures that teach and exhort us to do so are given below.

1 CORINTHIANS 14:4, JUDE 20 – *He who speaks in a tongue edifies himself... But you, beloved, building yourselves up on your most holy faith, praying in the Holy Spirit.*

The word 'edifies' means to build up something, the way a house is built up. A house is steadily built up by laying brick upon brick. Every time you pray in the spirit, layer upon layer of 'spiritual building material' is laid down in your inner man, resulting in your spirit being built up. Don't you want that?

The following analogy could not have been used in Paul's day, because batteries were not invented at that time. However, the effect of praying in tongues can be compared to the charging of a battery. People who pray at length in tongues will testify that their spirit gets charged up in the same way that a battery gets charged up. There are no flat batteries among those who pray at length in tongues. They are always charged up. There is no need for a 'kick start' with them. They are plugged in and speak at length in tongues and their spirit gets charged up. These kinds of people never find themselves needing encouragement from other Christians to get up and serve the Lord. Their batteries are always full.

If you want your inner man to be strong and robust, you must also build the Word of God into your spirit. To achieve this, you must have a regular diet of spirit food, which is the Word of God.

MATTHEW 4:4 – *But He answered and said, 'It is written, "Man shall not live by bread alone, but by every word that proceeds from the mouth of God."'*

It is as you meekly receive the Word (Jam. 1:21), study it, get illumination of it, meditate on it and act upon it, and pray at length in tongues, that your spirit will be built up. I teach this all the time, and I work at getting my hearers to follow this plan. As a result, those who obey end up having strong and sturdy spirits. They face up to all the adversities of life with the strength of the Lord.

Be Filled

If you want to be sensitive to what God wants to do in your life, you must be constantly filled with the Holy Spirit and with the Word of God. The Word of God expressly instructs Holy Spirit-baptized believers to be always filled with the Spirit.

EPHESIANS 5:18-21 – *And do not be drunk with wine, in which is dissipation; but be filled with the Spirit, speaking to one another in psalms and hymns and spiritual songs, singing and making melody in your heart to the Lord, giving thanks always for all things to God the Father in the name of our Lord Jesus Christ, submitting to one another in the fear of God.*

Paul wrote this epistle to Christians who had already been baptized in the Holy Spirit, and not to believers who were seeking to be baptized in the Spirit. It is reasonable to conclude that the Ephesian church must have been made up of Spirit-baptized believers because it was Paul's modus operandi to lead believers to be baptized in the Holy Spirit after they got saved (Acts 19:1-7).

To unpack the scripture above, first focus on the words 'be filled with the Spirit'. Those who just read the English translation of the phrase do not get the full import of the instruction. I am a serious student of the scriptures so, by using the Vine and Wuest commentaries on this passage of scripture, I dug deeper and I discovered the underlying Greek meaning of the phrase. The word 'filled' means, 'to fill up, to cause to abound, to furnish or supply liberally, to flood, to diffuse throughout' and the use of the particular verb 'be' in this scripture means that the 'being filled' should be an ongoing and continuous one. The instruction given to these Holy Spirit-baptized believers, therefore, was to 'be constantly filled, abounding in, having a liberal supply, flooded and diffused throughout with the Spirit'. This reminds me of the words of the Lord when He said, "Good measure, pressed down, shaken together and running over".

Now focus on the command, 'do not be drunk with wine'. This is set in contrast to the instruction to maintain a constant, overflowing presence of the Holy Spirit. The reason for this is that intoxication with alcohol hinders the believer from being filled with the Spirit of God. Take special note that the Holy Spirit was not giving the Ephesians permission to consume alcohol and the instruction was not a reference to the final effect of drinking strong drink. Many think that they can indulge in drinks that contain alcohol so long as they do not get to a point where they are so drunk that they find themselves stumbling about. The verb 'be' in the phrase 'be not drunk' is inceptive and this means that it expresses the beginning of an action. The command is therefore not to begin the process of becoming intoxicated.

Now, do not ignore the word dissipation. The word is not there by chance. It means, 'having a destructive effect'. Was Paul speaking about the destructive effect that alcohol has on the body of the believer? No, that could not be. It is clear that he was speaking about spiritual realities. The destructive effect is on the 'being filled with the Spirit'. The full phrase 'do not be drunk with wine, in which is dissipation but be filled with the Spirit' is more accurately understood as 'do not begin the process of becoming intoxicated with wine, because that has a negative effect on your working on being constantly filled with the Spirit'.

I will not drink wine or any other alcohol-based drink because I know that any degree, however small, of intoxication will hinder my ability to yield to the Spirit of God. Consuming any strong drink will throw my carefully built up tapestry of spiritual progress out of synchronization. It is obvious to me that I cannot yield to the effects of being filled with the Holy Spirit and the effects of being intoxicated with alcohol at the same time. I either yield to the effects of one glass of wine or maybe two, and perhaps three (as it usually progresses) and have my inhibitions artificially relaxed for a while, or I yield to the intoxication of being filled with the Spirit and engage in thanksgiving, praise and worship of the Lord in psalms, hymns and spiritual songs.

In order for you to maintain this constant infilling of the Holy Spirit, you should be constantly praying in tongues. Maintain and grow your two-hour sessions of praying in tongues and, whenever a convenient opportunity presents itself to you, pray in tongues. When you are alone, just open your mouth and pray in tongues. As you sit in or walk around your home, allow tongues to bubble out of your mouth. Pray in tongues when you drive your car about town. Any long-distance driving becomes a great opportunity for you to pray in tongues, so make use of it. This is how you maintain the fullness of the Spirit. Paul, who instructed the Ephesians to be constantly filled with the Spirit, prayed in tongues all the time. This is the secret. It is praying at length in tongues and whenever you can.

I also work on getting the fullness of the waters of the Spirit to seep into my spirit. This is hindered by my allowing carnality to remain in my life. The things that Paul wrote before he instructed them to be filled with the Spirit, are some of the things that I work on having removed from my life (Eph. 4:25-5:17).

Check out the scriptures surrounding his instruction to be filled with the Spirit. Paul's words, 'do not grieve the Holy Spirit of God', mean that nothing should be allowed to hinder the believer's progress in the Spirit. Constant heavy eating will block your being sensitive to the Spirit. Don't yield to gluttony but seek to travel light by living a fasted life. Work on getting rid of carnal thoughts and words, because out of the same mouth, tongues and cursing cannot come. It is one or the other. Sweet water or bitter water (Jam. 3:10-12).

As I said earlier, you must also be full of the Word of God. The two go together. The one cannot exist without the other.

COLOSSIANS 3:16-17 – *Let the word of Christ dwell in you richly in all wisdom, teaching and admonishing one another in psalms and hymns and spiritual songs, singing with grace in your hearts to the Lord. And whatever you do in word or deed, do all in the name of the Lord Jesus, giving thanks to God the Father through Him.*

Praying at length in tongues, getting rid of carnality and working on being filled with the Word will ensure a fullness of the Spirit and this is what is pleasing to God.

Drinking

The Spirit-baptized believer must maintain a constant fullness of the Spirit. The scripture says, 'be filled' – not partially filled but filled. We are not commanded to be one percent filled but to be one hundred percent filled. Ninety-nine percent filled is not filled. Filled means filled. This, and only this will result in an overflowing presence of the Holy Spirit.

In order to be filled with the Spirit you must drink of the waters of the Spirit. This drinking is similar to drinking natural water. In order to be filled with natural water you will have to drink more than a teaspoonful of water. One glass of water will not do. You will have to drink many glasses of water before you will be filled. Even then, after a few minutes, you will discover that there is space for more. The Lord Jesus Christ invited believers to come and drink of the waters of the Holy Spirit.

JOHN 7:37-39 – *On the last day, that great day of the feast, Jesus stood and cried out, saying, "If anyone thirsts, let him come to Me and drink. He who believes in Me, as the Scripture has said, out of his heart will flow rivers of living water." But this He spoke concerning the Spirit, whom those believing in Him would receive; for the Holy Spirit was not yet given, because Jesus was not yet glorified.*

This is how you drink of these waters. You pray in tongues. If you pray a little in tongues, you drink but a teaspoon of the waters of the Spirit. You will not be filled like that. A short stint in tongues represents perhaps half a glass. It is only when you pray at length in tongues repeatedly that you get filled to overflowing.

---

1 CORINTHIANS 12:13 – *For by one Spirit we were all baptized into one body whether Jews or Greeks, whether slaves or free and have all been made to drink into one Spirit.*

Paul used the same analogy of water that the Lord used. Why? Because the Spirit has qualities like water. When we first got baptized in the Holy Spirit we drank at the waters of life. We must continue now.

Fruit of the Spirit

Paul lists the constituents of the fruit of the Spirit in the fifth chapter of his letter to the Galatians. Notice that he does not use the plural form fruits but the singular. This points to the fact that each of the listed graces make up the whole. Kindness is part of love and so is long-suffering and so is goodness and gentleness and so on. Love is the fruit of the Spirit, and it is displayed in its impressive range of the parts of its whole.

GALATIANS 5:22-23 – *But the fruit of the Spirit is love, joy, peace, long-suffering, kindness, goodness, faithfulness, gentleness, self-control. Against such there is no law.*

The word fruit is used as a metaphor here to represent the thought, 'the result of the indwelling Spirit'. The phrase 'the fruit of the Spirit' should not be thought of as physical fruits such as apples, oranges and bananas. Those who have the fruit of the Spirit operative in their lives will have visible expressions of love, and all that constitutes it.

There are two ways that you can have the fruit of the Spirit operative in your life. One is through a diffusion of love and its parts coming from the Spirit as a baptism, and the other through acting on a steady leading of the Holy Spirit. Both have nothing to do with diligent human effort. It is all a product of the indwelling presence of the Spirit of God.

Character building such as the development of integrity, punctuality and etiquette is absolutely necessary in the life of a Christian, but this is not the fruit of the Spirit. These things need human effort and diligence to achieve.

If you build sessions of praying at length in tongues into your life, one day, while you are praying, you will hit a gusher of overwhelming love that will fill your whole being. This love of God has already been poured in your heart when you first got saved, but your prevailing in tongues is what opens the floodgates allowing this love to overwhelm you. When this happens to you, you will never be the same again. Love will become the ruling principle in your life. This is not human effort; it is as a result of the indwelling presence of God.

At another time you might hit a gusher of joy. Your whole heart will be flooded with joy. It will be, as someone sang, 'joy un-speakable and full of glory and the half has never yet been told'. This is not happiness that comes from a good life. It is the joy of the Lord (Neh. 8:10). No human effort here.

At another time, it might be the peace of God that will overwhelm you. This peace, as with all the other components of love, is beyond human understanding (Phil. 4:7). The Holy Spirit is the source of such peace.

In the second way in which you can have the fruit of the Spirit operative in your life, the Spirit of God brings forth love and all its attributes in a less spectacular, yet equally supernatural, way. This is achieved by a quiet leading of the Spirit-filled believer into practising a particular given portion of scripture.

JOHN 16:13 – *However, when He, the Spirit of truth, has come, He will guide you into all truth; for He will not speak on His own authority, but whatever He hears He will speak; and He will tell you things to come.*

If you pray at length in tongues, you will become sensitive to the guidance of the Holy Spirit. Amongst other things, He will guide you into the fruit of the Spirit. So, on a particular day, in response to something that someone might have done wrong to you, you might sense the Spirit saying to you, "Pay no attention to that suffered wrong". As you obey, a measure of the love of God will be released into your spirit.

At another time, you might sense Him saying, "Love is kind," or at another, "Love is not jealous," or at yet another, "Love is not easily provoked" (1 Cor. 13:4-7). This is His guidance into all truth and, if you obey, the agape love of God will seep into your spirit.

Through your praying at length in tongues, God will also deal with carnality that you persist in. It will be in your obedience that the love of God will be released in your spirit. The Holy Spirit's continual leading like this will eventually lead to the fruit of the Spirit being dominant in your life.

Now, I have noticed that those who are filled with the Holy Spirit and who speak at length in tongues find it impossible to hate, have bitterness, be critical, be selfish, gossip or whatever. They just can't do it. This is a result of the work of the Spirit done within their spirit while they were praying in tongues. This spiritual progress is achieved without the tongue-talking believer even being aware of what is happening in the spirit.

Finally, praying at length in tongues will elevate you into a dimension of love, joy, peace and the other parts of love that will amaze you. You will be like an eagle flying far above those who have not yielded to the Spirit in this way. They will be like sparrows struggling and fluttering around the gutters of life while you soar to greater heights using minimal effort through the torque of the Spirit that tongues has given you.

10 WORSHIP IN THE SPIRIT

New Dispensation

Believers under the New Covenant have been born again. They are the sons of God and the Holy Spirit dwells within them. If they reach out and receive the Baptism in the Holy Spirit, they enter into a spiritual dimension where they can worship God in the spirit. This is what the Father wants. God is a spirit and those who worship Him must worship Him in spirit and in truth. The Lord Jesus Christ introduced this thought to the woman of Samaria because soon thereafter it was to become a reality.

JOHN 4:23-24 – *But the hour is coming, and now is, when the true worshipers will worship the Father in spirit and truth; for the Father is seeking such to worship Him. God is Spirit, and those who worship Him must worship in spirit and truth.*

Holy Spirit-filled believers do not worship as believers did under the Old Covenant. Believers in those days worshipped God by physical means. They offered up burnt sacrifices, sweet-smelling incense and the like to God as a means of worship. David danced before the Lord with all his might. None of this is still applicable under the New Testament. We can only worship God in the Spirit. He wants us to bring spiritual sacrifices such as the anointed fruit of our lips, presenting our bodies as living sacrifices, dancing in the Spirit and worshipping Him through the perfect way of tongues.

The Perfect Way

There is no language on earth that can match the thanksgiving, praise and worship that is due to the living God. All our languages are the product of human reasoning and the longest surviving are but a few thousand years old. They are all imperfect and are nothing but flesh. The Lord Jesus Christ made it clear that 'that which is born of the flesh is flesh, and that which is born of the Spirit is spirit' (John 3:6). There are no terms and no adjectives in any of these languages that can express the rapturous and ecstatic praise that is due to the eternal God. Our earthly languages are only good for giving worship in the permissive will of God. We presume too much with our learned languages.

We need the perfect languages that come through the utterances given by the Holy Spirit if we are to rise up and match the worship that is due to the majestic One. Tongues constitute languages that have been untainted by the fallen human intellect.

When a believer worships in tongues, the human mind is set in a mode of quiescence while the Spirit selects words from the divine vocabulary to bring forth a perfect magnification of God. This is like when Adam was put to sleep while God formed Eve. Adam could not interfere with the perfect creating hand of God. Only tongues can bring the believer into true worship of the eternal God.

The human mind is finite. We know so little. Our knowledge of the past is clouded, and we believe history that has been written down for us by people who were influenced by their own motives and by their limited knowledge. The little that we know about the future is that which God has revealed to us and that we see but dimly, as through a mirror. We are limited to one place with our bodies and in our own ability we cannot heal a fly's knee. We then suppose that we can worship the omnipotent, omniscient, omnipresent and eternal God with such extreme limitations.

Only the Spirit of God can know what the perfect words for perfect worship are that each of the millions upon millions of Spirit-filled believers must release at a particular moment. The grand choir on earth and in heaven must be harmonized in perfect unity. Every note, every voice and every lyric must be synchronized by the Spirit to produce perfect worship. Only tongues can weave the glory of His omniscience, omnipresence and omnipotence into full celebration in one glorious song.

You don't have to remain in the impotent position that Charles Wesley found himself when he penned these words to his song: "O! For a thousand tongues to sing my dear Redeemer's praise! The glories of my God and King, the triumphs of His grace! My gracious Master and my God assist me to proclaim, to spread through all the world abroad, the honours of Thy name."

When you feel like this, know that tongues can come to your rescue. Assistance to express the honours of His name comes via tongues. Your extremity is the Holy Spirit's opportunity.

Yield to the Spirit and burst forth in tongues when you feel inexpressible gratitude for the goodness of God building up in you.

Doing this is the most perfect way of giving thanks to and blessing God. Many times when you are speaking in tongues, without you even knowing it you will be blessing and giving thanks to God in this most perfect way.

---

1 CORINTHIANS 14:16-17 – *Otherwise, if you bless with the spirit, how will he who occupies the place of the uninformed say "Amen" at your giving of thanks, since he does not understand what you say? For you indeed give thanks well, but the other is not edified.*

On the Day of Pentecost, when the Apostles and those who were with them first got filled with the Spirit, they spoke in other tongues as the Spirit gave them utterance. As they did that, they unknowingly were speaking the 'wonderful works of God' (Acts 2:11). This meant that they were expressing in glorious words the wonderful things that God had done, was doing or would yet do. No human being can know the depths of the glory of the works of God. Only the Spirit does and, when you worship God in tongues, He gives you superb words in tongues to express the glory of His works.

Cornelius and those in his home who believed the preaching of Peter, spoke in tongues and magnified God when they were filled with the Holy Spirit (Acts 10:46). This 'magnifying God' was an expression of the greatness of God in a known language that they had spoken in tongues. Spirit-filled believers will also do the same as the Spirit wills.

The Gift of Different Kinds of Tongues is the gateway to worshipping God in the Spirit. While speaking in an unknown tongue, the Spirit-filled believer breaks into psalms, hymns, spiritual songs and perfect melodies to express thanksgiving, praise and worship. As the

Spirit wills, the believer speaks or sings these in a known language. This happens through the simple gift of prophecy. Streams of words flow out of the spirit of the believer as he or she worships the Lord (Eph. 5:18-21 and Col. 3:16).

What is the conclusion then? The believer worships in an unknown tongue and worships in a known tongue (1 Cor. 14:15-17).

11 INCREASING THE ANOINTING

Before discussing how to increase the anointing, let us first consider what the anointing is. Anointing is a spiritual reality and is therefore not an easy concept to define. The scriptures do however give a type that teaches what the anointing is.

EXODUS 30:25 – *And you shall make from these a holy anointing oil, an ointment compounded according to the art of the perfumer. It shall be a holy anointing oil.*

Oil is a type of anointing. This helps us understand what the anointing is. The anointing is like oil. Natural oil has lubricating qualities that makes for easy movement. In like manner the anointing makes for easiness of spiritual operation. When someone is preaching, prophesying or teaching under the anointing there is an ease of flow. However, when the person is operating without the anointing it seems like a grind and a scraping. The people who are listening might not be able to define what the anointing is but will say, "no anointing".

The anointing also brings a measure of power (Acts 1:8) and gives a greater punch to preaching, to teaching and to all the other vocal gifts. It also gives the ability to accomplish the work of God. One needs the anointing to establish a church or any type of ministry.

All believers have an anointing. At the moment of being born again the Spirit takes residence in the new believer. His presence in the believer's spirit brings a measure of anointing.

---

1 JOHN 2:20, 27 – *But you have an anointing from the Holy One, and you know all things. But the anointing which you have received from Him abides in you, and you do not need that anyone teach you…but as the same anointing teaches you concerning all things, and is true, and is not a lie, and just as it has taught you, you will abide in Him.*

When and if the person gets baptized in the Holy Spirit, the anointing is greatly increased. A deeper anointing is immediately evident in the person's life.

ACTS 1:8 – *But you shall receive power when the Holy Spirit has come upon you; and you shall be witnesses to Me in Jerusalem, and in all Judea and Samaria, and to the end of the earth.*

There is an anointing that goes with each ministry. There is an anointing for an apostle, another for a prophet, another for an evangelist, another for a pastor and yet another for a teacher. For each of these ministries there is a unique anointing. The anointing is granted to the person at the time of the calling.

This anointing can be increased and can become heavier. The responsibility lies on the minister and not on the Lord to increase it. This increase of anointing is not simply received by asking the Lord to grant it. You must work on increasing the flow of the anointing.

If you pray at length in tongues, you tap into the oil of the Spirit (anointing) that is resident in the indwelling Spirit of God. This can be likened unto the pressing of olives in an olive-press. The more that olives go through the press, the more the oil that is produced. The more you pray for long stretches of time in tongues, the more anointing is produced.

The anointing is also increased when you spend time meditating on the Word. The anointing is in the Word and if you meditate on the Word rightly divided, then the oil oozes out into your spirit and becomes available for use.

When Tiffinny our daughter preached her maiden message, it was filled with power and anointing. Seasoned ministers who were present that day were stunned and said that there was no doubt that such preaching could only have come through someone who had spent time in the Word and who had prayed extensively in tongues. She testifies that she follows the principle I have shared here very closely.

Praying in your own language and meditating on teachings that seem to be correct but that have no emphasis in the New Covenant produces no anointing.

12 SPIRITUAL WARFARE

The Good Fight

Those who pray in the Spirit will have to fight to keep themselves in that space. You can be sure of that. There is going to be a battle before there is victory. Your flesh does not want you to pray in tongues, the devil does not want you to pray in tongues, and the world does not want you to pray in tongues. You have a battle on your hands and that is why the scriptures encourage you to fight the good fight of faith.

---

1 TIMOTHY 6:12 – *Fight the good fight of faith, lay hold on eternal life, to which you were also called and have confessed the good confession in the presence of many witnesses.*

Keep the fight in the arena of faith and it will remain a good one to behold. Those in the grandstands of heaven and those on the earth will rejoice at your victories. If you keep yourself in faith, you will be victorious over the flesh, over the devil and over the world, every time.

Romans 8:32 – *Yet in all these things we are more than conquerors through Him who loved us.*

If the flesh is geared against your entering into praying in your understanding, how much more is it set against your praying in the spirit? The flesh is positioned against the Spirit of God, and the Spirit of God against the flesh. They are in direct opposition to one another. The flesh desires to have dominion over your decisions, while the Holy Spirit has a passionate desire to bring you under His guidance. The battle between the flesh and the Spirit will never cease (Gal. 5:17).

The flesh just wants to eat and eat, drink and drink, be tired and be tired, be lazy and be lazy, sleep and sleep, yawn and yawn, make excuses and make excuses, envy and envy, be angry and be angry, gossip and gossip, fear and fear and swear and swear. It only wants to mope and groan, throw pity parties, hate people, tell lies and indulge in useless feelings. Refuse to listen to it. Your will is the deciding power. You can decide in favour of the carnal and yield to the flesh, or you can decide in favour of the Spirit and pray in tongues. Decide for praying in tongues and stick with it because, if you don't, the flesh will keep you on an emotional roller-coaster. Remember that, where the flesh is strong, the devil and his demons can have a field day.

Satan and all his demons are also set against your praying in the Holy Spirit. Past experience has taught them that, if they allow you to prevail in tongues, multitudes will be released from their clutches. If you start taking praying in tongues seriously, the devil will send his top agents to stop you. They will use different strategies. One of these is to inject floods of evil thoughts into your mind. Another one is to scream in your ears, insisting that you are wasting your time and yet another is to whisper incessantly in your precious ears that you are just speaking nothing but gibberish.

Don't listen to them or nurse their thoughts. They are all liars. Rise up with authority, and in the name of Jesus Christ, and command these evil spirits to go and they will. If all fails, the Evil One will come himself. Although he knows that he is a defeated foe, he will take his chances. Knock him squarely on his nose by your confession of the Word and resist him steadfastly in the faith and he will flee in terror from you (1 Pet. 5:8-9 and Jam. 4:7).

The whole world system is also set against the things of the Spirit. It is a great big strategy to block us from getting interested in things pertaining to the Spirit of God. It is designed to *entrance* the dwellers upon the earth. Some of these things are legitimate, such as sports, cars, travel, nature, study, business and the like. However, these things are kept before the believer in such a way as to completely captivate him or her, so that they are distracted from moving in things concerning the Spirit. The strength and continuous call of television and the internet blocks the desire to pray in the Holy Spirit. Believers get to the place where they say, "I have no time for tongues," and the world gets the upper hand (1 John 2:15-17). Decide in favour of tongues and not to yield to the world and all its fascinations. Operate in faith and you will overcome the world (1 John 5:4).

The main ingredient of the good fight of faith is, of course, faith itself. What you need then is faith. The bible is clear on how you get it. Faith comes by hearing, and hearing by the Word of God. Locate scriptures in the bible that relate to speaking in tongues and read them, meditate on them, confess them and act on them, and your faith will grow in leaps and bounds. The scriptures relating to praying in the Spirit must dwell in you richly and you must always be bubbling over in tongues, giving the Spirit free sway, and you will become untouchable.

Over the years I have realized that there is always a danger of a relapse. When the initial excitement of the possibilities of victory in the Spirit wears off, then there is a pull back to the old life. If you recognize that you are falling back, rise up and fight the good fight of faith, claiming your position that you had in prayer.

It is not going to be easy. Praying in tongues is like rowing a boat against the flow of the current. To overcome the resistance of the waters you must just continue to row and use strength to overcome. If you persist, you will overcome and eventually get to your destination. Remember that there are calmer waters upstream.

Strong in the Lord

The devil and all his demons have been defeated by the Lord Jesus Christ in His work of redemption two thousand years ago. He is the victor and we are the triumphant church.

COLOSSIANS 2:15 – *Having disarmed principalities and powers, He made a public spectacle of them, triumphing over them in it.*

However, that is not all that the bible has to say on the subject. So, don't think that, because the devil and his demons have been defeated, there is nothing for you to do any further in regard to them. There is strong opposition coming from that quarter (Eph. 6:12). Rebuking them from time to time, simply ignoring them or saying that they are defeated foes, will not do. It is our responsibility to protect ourselves against all their attacks, to stand against their opposition and to enforce their defeat. Paul, inspired by the Spirit of God, gave the following instructions in this regard.

EPHESIANS 6:10-11 – *Finally, my brethren, be strong in the Lord and in the power of His might. Put on the whole armour of God, that you may be able to stand against the wiles of the devil.*

The instruction 'be strong in the Lord and in the power of His might' was not an exhortation for them to use their own power or their own ability, nor was it an encouragement to self-effort in any way, shape, form or fashion. Their strength was to be 'in the Lord' and in the power 'of His might'. The strength and power that Paul was speaking about was to be of divine origin.

When this letter, written in Greek, was first read by the Ephesians, they understood exactly what Paul was saying. Unfortunately, the poor English translation of this verse that we read obscures the true meaning of the exhortation. It is, therefore, imperative that believers know the Greek meaning of three key words in this portion of scripture. If they don't, the full meaning of Paul's exhortation, will remain buried in the Greek.

'Be strong' is *endunamoo* and means 'be continually clothed with strength, as a person would put on a garment'. 'Power' is *kratos* and means 'manifested power'. 'Might' is *ischuos* and means 'inherent power' (Wuest Eph. 6:12). The Ephesians were instructed through these words to continually clothe themselves with the inherent and manifesting power of God.

All three words are associated with Holy Spirit power and point us back to the instructions that the Lord Jesus Christ gave to His disciples after His resurrection. At one meeting with them, He commanded them to wait in Jerusalem until they were endued (clothed) with power from heaven (Luke 24:49) and at another He assured them that they would receive power after the Holy Spirit came upon them (Acts 1:8).

This clothing of yourself with Holy Spirit power can only be achieved by your praying at length in tongues. How else will it be done? Keep on with your two-hour sessions of praying in tongues, and you will clothe yourself with the anointing as one would put on a garment.

Further to this, whether you realize it or not, the power of God will be manifesting as bolts of lightning through you. At your approach, demons will scream out in terror, because they were defeated by this very power when God raised Christ Jesus from the dead.

Many years ago, I led a number of believers to an informal settlement made up of mainly wood and iron shacks, to witness to the people who lived there. As we went from door to door, sharing the gospel, we heard screams of terror coming from somewhere ahead of us. We wondered what was happening. As we got closer, the screams intensified. Eventually, we got to the shack out of which the screams were coming. When we opened the door and looked inside, we discovered that it was a young, wide-eyed girl, of about sixteen years old, who was screaming with such terror. The girl was cowering in a corner, full of fear, and was begging us to go. We realized that she was demon-possessed and that it was really the demons who were in her that were screaming out in fear. We then took her to a nearby large house, led her to the Lord and then began to cast out the demons. It is amazing, but true, that when we commanded the demons to come out, she was lifted about knee height off the floor and went flying across the room, ending up on the far side of the room. We then scurried over to her, held her down and commanded the demons to come out until she was free and in her right mind.

She then told us that earlier, without her knowing that we were approaching the shack, she felt power hit her like bolts of lightning, throwing her about and that, when we were casting out the demons, it was an incredible power that drove them out. While she was sitting in her right mind and speaking to us, three angry men burst into the room and shouted at us for driving the demons out of her. After they left, some bystanders told us that these men used her in witchcraft matters and made much money out of her demonic spiritual abilities (Acts 16:19).

Discussing it later, we realized that we were about fifty metres away from her shack when we first heard the screams. There was no doubt in our minds that it was the manifest Holy Spirit power that caused the demons to scream out in terror. We never felt the power and were totally unaware that it was manifesting through us. However, this we knew: that power was manifest because we were always praying for hours in tongues.

Armour of God

Despite the fact that you can and must continually clothe yourself with the inherent and manifesting power of God, you will still be a target for the devil and his cohorts. This is why, in addition to the previous exhortation, we are also instructed to put on the whole armour of God, so that we may be able to withstand the devil and any demon when we are attacked by him or them.

EPHESIANS 6:13 – *Therefore take up the whole armour of God, that you may be able to withstand in the evil day, and having done all, to stand.*

In this world you will find yourself in close combat with wicked forces of darkness. The four categories that we have to deal with are principalities, powers, rulers of the darkness of this age and spiritual hosts of wickedness in the heavenly places (Eph. 6:12). They are on constant attack and want you to fall. The devil himself will shoot a fiery dart towards you. They also have devious and cunning strategies and manoeuvres designed to get you to do their will. In order to be protected against these demonic assaults, you must put on the whole armour of God.

EPHESIANS 6:14-17 – *Stand therefore, having girded your waist with truth, having put on the breastplate of righteousness, and having shod your feet with the preparation of the gospel of peace; above all, taking the shield of faith with which you will be able to quench all the fiery darts of the wicked one. And take the helmet of salvation, and the sword of the Spirit, which is the word of God;*

The question is, how will we do that? Must we go into our rooms and say, "I now put on the Breast Plate of Righteousness," and then make the actions of putting that on? Must we then say, "I now put on the Belt of Truth," and then make the actions of tying a belt? Must we do the same with every piece of armour?

My response to these questions are questions as well. Does the above sound right to you? Is the armour not spiritual? Will the devil not laugh at such actions? Of course, he will, because these are ridiculous efforts to protect ourselves from his pernicious attacks. The devil and his demons are spirits and the armour must be of a spiritual materiality if it is to be effective. Does that not make sense?

This is how you put on the armour of God. You must pray at length in tongues and obey the Lord in the scriptures relating to that piece of the armour of God and, as you do that, the breast plate of righteousness, the belt of truth, the shield of faith, the helmet of salvation, the gospel shoes, the cloak of zeal and the sword of the Spirit will form around you (Eph. 6:13-17).

Several years ago, our church dedicated a number of days to fasting and praying. On the Sunday afternoon, the last day of our fast, there were about eighty people who had gathered for prayer. We were all in one accord, praying in tongues, when my wife had a manifestation of the gift of Discerning of Spirits. Seeing into the spirit realm, she saw the intercessors walking about with the armour of God formed around them and particularly prominent was the cloak of zeal. The Holy Spirit was showing that it was as a result of them praying for days in tongues.

The more you pray in the Spirit, the more untouchable you become. So, get yourself into a position of 'untouchableness'.

Wicked Spirits Above

Christians do not only have to deal with demonic forces that are upon the earth; they also have to contend with wicked spirits in the spiritual atmosphere above the earth. These are the demonic forces that are referred to as 'spiritual hosts of wickedness in the heavenly places'.

EPHESIANS 6:12 – *For we do not wrestle against flesh and blood, but against principalities, against powers, against the rulers of the darkness of this age, against spiritual hosts of wickedness in the heavenly places.*

The word hosts in the scripture above is another word for armies. These wicked spirits are therefore organized armies that operate in the heavenlies. They have to be dealt with if you are to have victory.

If the Lord opens your spiritual eyes while you are praying in tongues, you will see a thick, dark cloud way up in the heavens. However, on closer examination, you will realize that it is not a dark cloud at all, but wicked spirits in close proximity and tightly intertwined, who are trying to block your prayers. If you persist in praying in tongues, the dense cloud will begin to melt like wax, and you will burn a hole through it. If you continue pressing in, by virtue of your focused praying in tongues an open heaven will develop above you. You will then have great liberty in prayer. Your prayers, both in the Spirit and in the understanding, will shoot up to the throne unhindered.

Spiritual insight into how these wicked spirits in the heavens operate is given to us in the account of Daniel when he was fasting and praying for three weeks. Demonic forces were blocking the answer to his prayer.

DANIEL 10:12-13 – *Then he said to me, "Do not fear, Daniel, for from the first day that you set your heart to understand, and to humble yourself before your God, your words were heard; and I have come because of your words. But the prince of the kingdom of Persia withstood me twenty-one days; and behold, Michael, one of the chief princes, came to help me, for I had been left alone there with the kings of Persia."*

Prayers in your learned language will have a hard time breaking through the ranks of these wicked armies in the spiritual realm above us. It is only the power of the Spirit of God that can break through with ease.

The church must also engage herself collectively in praying in the spirit. As they pray in the tongues, the church drives back the forces of darkness in the heavenlies, but when they slack these demons gain ground against them. It's like a sword fight going back and forth.

An excellent illustration of this is given in the account of Israel, when the nation was fighting against the peoples of Amalek (Ex. 17:1-6). When Moses' hands were held up, then Israel prevailed, and when his hands were down, then the enemy prevailed. Likewise, when we pray in the spirit the armies of heaven push the forces of darkness back. When we slack in praying in the spirit, the forces of darkness get the upper hand. This happens whether we sense it or not. There is always warfare in the spiritual world.

The believer has another front of the battle to deal with. There are strongholds that must be pulled down, arguments and high things that exalt themselves above the knowledge of God that must be cast down, and thoughts that must be brought into obedience to Christ (2 Cor. 10:3-5).

These are all thought patterns in the minds of people that have been developed there through their yielding to doctrines of demons over a period of time. There are a host of them. Examples are Islam, Mormonism, Evolutionism, Mafias, Pseudo-Christian religions and the like. Demons set themselves up in these minds, developing strongholds. Without purposefully targeting these strongholds, the believer just engages in praying in tongues and, in the process, these foundations of traditions that have been there for generations come tumbling down.

Spiritual warfare has nothing at all to do with the strange antics that some Christians get up to. Some try to use 'warring tongues' to shoot spiritual missiles at demonic forces to torment and defeat them. Some wear combat clothing and try to appear as an army fighting against Satan. Others want to get into airplanes and try to attack the forces of darkness from there. They forget that the Lord had total victory while walking on the earth and Paul and Silas were in the dungeon, chained down, when the power of God was manifest. "It is not by might nor by power but by My Spirit," says the Lord.

13 PRAYING WITH THE UNDERSTANDING

This book is about praying in the Spirit. However, while the Spirit is careful to remind us that we must pray in tongues, there is also much exhortation and teaching in the scriptures on praying with the understanding. Paul gives us a peek into his own prayer life and shows us how it is done. Some of his prayers were in an unknown language, and some were with his understanding.

---

1 CORINTHIANS 14:15 – *What is the conclusion then? I will pray with the spirit, and I will also pray with the understanding. I will sing with the spirit, and I will also sing with the understanding.*

In fact, if believers want to be effective in their prayer lives, they will have to pray all types of prayers. Different types of prayer are taught in the bible. There is the Prayer of Faith, the Prayer of Commitment and the Prayer of Consecration, to mention but a few.

EPHESIANS 6:18 – *praying always with all prayer and supplication in the Spirit, being watchful to this end with all perseverance and supplication for all the saints*

All prayer in the understanding must be in line with the scriptures (John 15:7). It is to the degree of accuracy of praying in line with the scriptures that our prayers will be in line with the mind of God. When we are praying the various types of prayers – or if we are supplicating, interceding or giving thanks, praise and worship – we must be careful to keep these in accordance with the Word of God. This is not praying in the Spirit, but these prayers are in the spirit of His Word. There is a difference.

There are also Word-based prayers that we can pray and, because these prayers are recorded in the scriptures, they have been inspired by the Spirit. So, when we pray these prayers we are praying in line with the Spirit of God. Two of these prayers have been given to us in the Book of Ephesians. The first one is found in the first chapter. Paul prayed that the Father would give the saints at Ephesus the spirit of wisdom and revelation in the knowledge of Him, and that He would enlighten the eyes of their understanding so that they could have revelation of what God had provided for them in the New Covenant (Eph. 1:15-23). In the third chapter, Paul prays that the Father would grant the believers strength, knowledge of the indwelling Christ and a revelation of love (Eph. 3:14-19). These entire prayers must be read, studied, meditated upon, spoken out and acted upon, and then we will have anointed prayers in the understanding.

I always know that I am praying perfectly in line with the will of God when I pray these prayers and others given in the epistles. This is how I do it. I read these scriptures, study and meditate on them. Then, sometimes I keep the bible open to these verses and pray them directly from the bible. At other times I pray them directly from my inner man, where they are lodged. I teach the church to do the same, and together we grow in grace and in the knowledge of Jesus Christ our Lord.

There are also Spirit-directed prayers. Sometimes the Holy Spirit gives us direction on what to pray for. He might by a leading, a word of wisdom, a vision or a dream guide us on what or whom to pray for. This will lead to praying in the understanding, but also praying in tongues.

When praying in the Spirit, sometimes we find ourselves praying words that are in our learned language, but that are flowing out of our spirits. These are prayers that are being prayed through the simple gift of prophecy and are perfectly in line with the will of God.

It is God's plan for us to pray both with the Spirit and with the understanding, but when we pray in the understanding our praying must be according to His Word.

If a believer only prays in the understanding, then the spirit of that person will feel like someone feels when they are short-changed. They feel robbed and also disappointed in the person who has cheated them. The spirit of the person will always be left unhappy that it was left out of the business. It will be grieved and remain grieved until it gets involved in the praying. However, when the person has been baptized in the Holy Spirit and continues in a life of speaking in tongues, that feeling will be eradicated because the spirit will feel content after your session of prayer.

14 SAYINGS

Praying at length in tongues is not new to the church. People have always yielded to the Holy Spirit in this way. However, the time for the restoration of it, and the spread of the discipline among all believers, is now.

A few examples, from the many that we could have used, are given below. This is to show you that others who have lived before us also embraced the right and privilege given to them by the Lord when He said, 'In My name you will speak in tongues...' (Mark 16:17).

Paul, the great apostle said, 'I thank my God I speak with tongues more than you all'. If you read the twelfth, thirteen and fourteenth chapters of Paul's first letter to the Corinthians, you will discover that Paul did not write these words to a people who did not know about the Holy Spirit. The Corinthians had many manifestations of the gifts of the Spirit and spoke in tongues to such an extent that their use of the gift had to be regulated. Yet, Paul said that he spoke in tongues more than all of them. This can only mean that Paul prayed for long hours in tongues.

Jude, in his short letter wrote, "But you, beloved, building yourselves up on your most holy faith, praying in the Holy Spirit". Jude instructs the believers to pray in the Holy Spirit, because in doing so they would be spiritually edifying themselves. Praying for an extended period of time is implied in the words, 'building yourselves up'. Building up takes time. It is no ten-minute job. Then he himself must have been a person who prayed at length in tongues. How else would he have the boldness to teach others to pray in the Spirit if he did not do so?

John G Lake was mightily used by the Lord at the turn of the twentieth century. Gifts of the Spirit manifested in His life on a regular basis. He said, "I want to talk with the utmost frankness and say to you that tongues have been the making of my ministry. It is that peculiar communication with God, when God reveals to my soul the truth that I utter to you day by day in the ministry. Many times, I climb out of bed, take my pencil and pad, and jot down the beautiful things of God, the wonderful things of God that He talks out in my spirit and reveals to my heart." This kind of talk comes from praying at length in tongues.

Smith Wigglesworth also had an above the ordinary miraculous ministry during the first half of the 1900s. He was a man who prayed for extended periods. Of praying in tongues he said, "No Pentecostal person ought to get out of bed without being lost in the Spirit and speaking in tongues as the Spirit gives utterance. No one should come into the door of an assembly without speaking in tongues or having a psalm, or a note of praise. We emphasize that, at the incoming of the Spirit, He should so fill us that the last member in the body is yielded to Him, and that no one is baptized in the Spirit without speaking in tongues, as the Spirit gives utterance; and I maintain that, with a constant filling, you will speak in tongues morning, noon and night. As you live in the Spirit, when you walk down the steps of the house where you live the devil will have to go before you. You will be more than a conqueror over the devil. I see everything a failure except that which is done in the Spirit. But as you live in the Spirit, you move, act, eat, drink, and do everything to the glory of God."

Howard Carter, who played a major role in establishing the Pentecostal movement in Great Britain and ministering worldwide on things pertaining to the Holy Spirit said, "We must not forget that speaking with other tongues is not only the initial evidence of the Holy Spirit's infilling, but it is a continual experience for the rest of one's life to assist us in the worship of God… Speaking in tongues is a flowing stream that should never dry up and that will enrich one's life spiritually."

Oral Roberts, who was on the forefront of the Healing Revival of the 1950s, went on to build a great university and hospital and had a very dynamic and extensive ministry that stretched from the forties into the nineties. He wrote, "You and I must learn to pray from the river within us, not from the neck up and not from the lips. We've got to get down deep into the river, into the subterranean area, because the river is flowing! A mighty river is flowing day and night, twenty-four hours a day, seven days a week, reaching all the way up to heaven in spiritual communicating with God!"

Kenneth Hagin ministered for almost seventy years before he was translated to heaven in 2003. I have no doubt that he was the greatest prophet to emerge in the twentieth century. He said, "Our message is always this, 'Be filled with the Spirit. This is God's place for you, and it is as far above the natural life as the heavens are above the earth. Yield yourselves for God to fill… However, I have found that this extra measure of the Holy Spirit operates in my life only if I follow the practice of continually praying daily in tongues… In fact, the greatest things that ever happened to me in my walk with God came as a result of praying with other tongues… I'll say it again – the primary knowledge I've gained from the bible, I didn't get by reading someone's book. The deeper things of the Word of God I learned on my knees praying in other tongues."

If we want the results and the resting upon us of the greater weight of glory it will do us good to be followers of those who inherit the promises of God (Heb. 6:12).

15 THE SECRET PLACE OF THE MOST HIGH

Go for the genuine thing. I have set out the path to victory clearly for you. Abandon smooth talk and winds of doctrine that promise you victory but yield no results. Extended times of praying in tongues together with Spirit-inspired and Spirit-directed prayer, infused and followed by faith, trust, obedience and patience, all undergirded by love produces stunning results. This is the way to go.

Your foremost priority is to set up the secret place of the Most High in your life. This is your daily entrance into His presence that eventually gets established as your intimate fellowship and indispensable time of doing business with the Father.

PSALM 91:1 – *He who dwells in the secret place of the Most High Shall abide under the shadow of the Almighty.*

The secret place of the Most High is of the utmost importance. Your successful flowing in it will bypass all the supposedly wonderful solutions that are preached. All God's servants should be discipling His people into this, His top priority for their all-round success. There are no short cuts. This is it.

Get started immediately. Build up the secret place of the Most High in your life. To achieve this, start by praying at length in tongues when in your prayer closet. This must cover the bulk of your time when in prayer. You must also include times of praying in the understanding, fellowship, worship and study of the scriptures as directed earlier in this book.

The foundation of the secret place of the Most High is His Word. You must have solid times of studying the scriptures, either immediately before entering into prayer or some time before. All prayer must have a solid foundation in the Word. The Lord said that if we abide in Him, and His words abide in us, we will ask what we desire, and these things would be done for us (John 15:7).

At your selected time to study the Word, enter your prayer closet with your bible, a pen and a book to write in. Sit in your favourite chair and choose a subject to study. You can take this book with you and use it as your basis for study because it covers a great deal of things relating to the Spirit. Dig into the scriptures using a concordance and other bible tools and it won't be long before you will find yourself 'chasing a rabbit'. By this I mean that as you study one scripture so will you be led to another and to another until the Word becomes a fire burning in your bones.

JEREMIAH 20:9 – *Then I said, "I will not make mention of Him, Nor speak anymore in His name." But His word was in my heart like a burning fire shut up in my bones; I was weary of holding it back, And I could not.*

Do the above. Don't underestimate the study of His Word. This is absolutely necessary for the Father to increase His speed in working for you. After a while this will become part of you and the foundation for success will have been laid in your life.

You further build up the secret place of the Most High in your life by praying at length in tongues. So, when your time comes for prayer, go into your prayer room, shut the door behind you and lift up holy hands and just begin to pray in tongues. Don't even touch your own language as you aim for two hours of praying in tongues. This is speaking to God whether your friend believes this to be true or not. Such kind of praying always produces Holy Spirit results.

During your times of praying in tongues the Lord will show you things that relate to His plan and purpose for your life. This will lead to you praying about these things in your understanding. These are *Spirit-directed* prayers. These prayers will all help to propel you into His plan and purpose for your life.

Also spend time praying *Spirit-inspired* prayers. These are prayers that are recorded in the bible. The scriptures are all inspired and if a prayer is recorded in the bible that means that the writer was inspired to write those words. Examples of these are the ones that Paul prayed for the Ephesian believers that are found in the first and third chapters of his letter to them. Pray these prayers regularly and your spiritual progress will be evident for all to see.

The Holy Spirit guides you into all truth. There are scriptures that deal with prayer, giving, forgiveness and so forth. These must be built into your life through faith, trust, obedience, patience and love. The bold confession that follows your time spent in the secret place will lead to these Spirit-produced blessings becoming a reality in your life.

The secret place of the Most High is a wonderful place to be in. At times it is pure fellowship with the Father that leads to 'joy unspeakable, full of glory and the half has never yet been told'. At other times it will be thanksgiving, praise and worship of the living God.

All of the above will build up the secret place of the Most High in your life that will result in you abiding under the shadow of the Most High. In His presence is fullness of joy and at His right hand are pleasures for evermore.

This is the way to go. If you choose this path and if you are diligent in it, you will break through into the blessings that come directly from the gracious hand of God. Despite what other people say and what the flesh, the devil and the world might say, you will be on a path to a sure reward.

MATTHEW 6:6 – *But you, when you pray, go into your room, and when you have shut your door, pray to your Father who is in the secret place; and your Father who sees in secret will reward you openly.*

Put your confidence in God and pray about everything that concerns you. If you are married, pray for your spouse; if you have children, pray for them; pray for other family members; pray for the believers and pray for your pastor. Pray all kinds of prayers. Take all things great and small to prayer.

Let His Word fully persuaded you, obey Him in all things, trusting Him to do what He promised, and wait patiently for the fulfilment of these, all the while walking in love and forgiving all those who do you wrong. Live in peace with all as far as it is possible with you.

Do these things and the great God of Abraham, Isaac and Jacob, who is the God and Father of our Lord Jesus Christ and is your God and your Father, will break through into your life as the morning sun rises and gives life to this world.

PART TWO

SCRIPTURAL BASIS

1 BEGINNINGS OF TONGUES

Revelations in the Old Testament

There are some scriptures in the Law and the Prophets that make direct reference to speaking in tongues, while others are somewhat veiled. Those who are filled with the Holy Spirit know that these refer to speaking in tongues.

---

2 PETER 1:20-21 – *Knowing this first, that no prophecy of Scripture is of any private interpretation, for prophecy never came by the will of man, but holy men of God spoke as they were moved by the Holy Spirit.*

Things that became a reality under the New Covenant were first revealed in the Law and the Prophets, as the Lord described what is known to us as the Old Testament. The prophets of old were inspired by the Spirit to write what they wrote and, in most cases, did not even know the prophetic nature of their writings.

---

1 PETER 1:19 – *And so we have the prophetic word confirmed, which you do well to heed as a light that shines in a dark place, until the day dawns and the morning star rises in your hearts*

Job, in one of his discourses said, "Men listened to me and waited, and kept silence for my counsel. After my words they did not speak again, and my speech settled on them as dew. They waited for me as for the rain, and they opened their mouth wide as for the spring rain" (Job 29:21-23). This scripture has a double meaning.

First, Job speaks about how people respected and revered him while he was doing well. A most beautiful scripture describing the reaction of people in the presence of a man or woman of God, who is highly esteemed in their sight.

Second, there is a prophetic reference to tongues in his words. Job was unaware of this. The prophetic insight of this portion of scripture could be understood as follows. When believers are in the presence of God, they listen and wait upon Him. His Word gets illuminated and they get direction on what they should do in life and, when they get it, they fully accept His counsel. In His presence, they are always in great anticipation (open their mouths wide) of being filled with the Holy Spirit. In this kind of setting, people get filled with the Holy Spirit and His speech (tongues) settles on them, and they speak these words out. 'Dew', 'rain' and 'spring rain' are all types of the Holy Spirit.

God spoke through Solomon and said, "Turn at My rebuke; Surely I will pour out My Spirit on you; I will make My words known to you" (Prov. 1:23). These words also have a double meaning.

Solomon personifies wisdom in this portion of scripture. Wisdom rebukes the fool and promises to pour his spirit on the person who heeds the rebuke and to reveal wisdom unto him or her.

However, there is revelation on speaking in tongues in these words too. 'Turn at My rebuke' is God calling the sinner to repentance. 'Surely I will pour My Spirit on you' is a definite promise of the Baptism in the Holy Spirit. 'I will make My words known to you' refers to tongues and interpretation of tongues.

Isaiah wrote, "For with stammering lips and another tongue, He will speak to this people..." This is a reference to tongues and Paul says so in his first letter to the Corinthians (Is. 28:11 and 1 Cor. 14:21).

Again, God, speaking through Joel the prophet, promised that there was a time coming when He would pour out His Spirit on all flesh. At that time His sons (menservants) and His daughters (maidservants) would prophesy, and the old men would dream dreams and the young men would see visions (Joel 2:28-29). This is a clear reference to the Baptism in the Holy Spirit. Peter quoted this scripture in his preaching, on the Day of Pentecost, when the apostles and others got filled with the Holy Spirit and spoke in other tongues. He said that their Baptism in the Holy Spirit and their speaking in tongues was a fulfilment of Joel's prophecy, saying, "This is what was spoken by the prophet Joel" (Acts 2:16).

Although no believer actually spoke in tongues during the days of the Law and the Prophets, there is enough revelation in the scriptures that proves that this was coming and was part of God's plan and purpose for His church.

The Lord's Praying in Tongues

Some believe that the Lord did not pray in tongues while He was upon the earth and some believe that He did. I will not be dogmatic on either of the two views but will set down both for you to consider. This study on Different Kinds of Tongues would be incomplete if I was completely silent on the matter.

View 1: The Lord did not Speak in Tongues

The Lord Jesus Christ never spoke in tongues when He was upon the earth. There is no place in the bible that says that He spoke in tongues. All His praying was in His own understanding. The reasons for this are given below.

First, the Lord Jesus Christ operated under the Old Covenant. He could never have spoken in tongues because the gifts of Different Kind of Tongues and Interpretation of Tongues were reserved exclusively for those who lived under the New Covenant.

ROMANS 15:8 – *Now I say that Jesus Christ has become a servant to the circumcision for the truth of God, to confirm the promises made to the fathers...*

Second, if the initial evidence of the Baptism in the Holy Spirit is speaking in tongues, then this was not manifested when the Lord was filled with the Holy Spirit. He was filled with the Holy Spirit (Luke 4:1) but He never spoke in tongues at that moment as believers did in various places in the Book of Acts.

LUKE 3:21-22 – *When all the people were baptized, it came to pass that Jesus also was baptized; and while He prayed, the heaven was opened. And the Holy Spirit descended in bodily form like a dove upon Him, and a voice came from heaven which said, "You are My beloved Son; in You I am well pleased."*

The phrases 'groaned in the spirit and was troubled' and 'groaning in Himself' (John 11:33,38) do not make reference to tongues. These words simply refer to the Lord's grief and compassion.

View 2: The Lord did Speak in Tongues

The Lord Jesus Christ did speak in tongues (in His private prayer life) when He was upon the earth. Although there is no place in the bible where it specifically says that the Lord spoke in tongues, there is clear reference in the Book of John that He did.

JOHN 11:33,38 – *Therefore, when Jesus saw her weeping, and the Jews who came with her weeping, He groaned in the spirit and was troubled... Then Jesus, again groaning in Himself, came to the tomb.*

In the scripture given above, the lower case is used for the 's' in the word 'spirit' but the translators should rather have rendered the phrase 'groaned in the Spirit' using the upper case for the 's' because the context points to a work of the Spirit of God. That groaning in this manner is a manifestation of the Holy Spirit is made clear by Paul's letter to the Romans.

Paul told the Romans that when they were in prayer and experienced *'groanings which cannot be uttered'* this was actually the Holy Spirit making intercession through them in inarticulate speech (Rom. 8:26). This is deep praying in tongues. Paul also told the Romans that 'the Spirit helps in our weaknesses'. Vine's tells us that the Greek meaning of word 'helps' is 'to take hold together with'. Paul was therefore telling these believers that, when they found themselves groaning in the Spirit, it was in fact the Spirit of God that was joining in with them and helping them to roll away heavy burdens through the medium of supernatural prayer.

Returning to the scene that was playing out before the tomb of Lazarus, it can never be that the Lord was grieving for Lazarus because He was fully persuaded that He would raise him from the dead. Of course, the Lord was moved with compassion at the suffering of those around Him, but it was this very compassion that triggered the move of the Spirit in Him, as it did at other times, when He healed the multitudes (Matt. 14:14). As the Holy Spirit moved in Him, the Lord began to groan in the Spirit. In the light of what Paul taught later, we know that these groans were intercessions that could not be articulated in a known language (Vine's: groanings) and was the Holy Spirit helping Him to roll away the heavy burden of death. This is the highest level of praying in tongues and the deepest intercession.

John also wrote that the Lord was 'troubled'. An accurate translation of this word is 'He troubled Himself'. The pushing up of the groans of the Spirit of God in the Lord is described by John as Him being troubled. Troubled by what? All along, since hearing of the news of Lazarus' death, the Lord was walking in the highest form of faith saying, "Lazarus is not dead but sleeping," and "Your brother will rise again," and "I am the resurrection and the life". The Lord 'troubling Himself' was not grief but was deep praying in the Spirit by someone who was accustomed to such praying. This was not a first-time surprise happening for the Lord. If this miracle needed this kind of prayer, then so did others. The Lord, no doubt, found Himself yielding to the Holy Spirit in this manner when praying in private. He always knew that the Father heard Him, because His Holy Spirit intercession in private preceded His public miracles.

Although the divine record does not say that the Lord spoke in tongues when the Spirit of God came upon Him in the River Jordan, it must be that He released the pent-up pressure of tongues on His way to the wilderness. This position is taken because it is inconceivable that He who had received the fullness of the Spirit (John 3:34) would be limited to the lowly Hebrew, Aramaic or koine Greek in His communicating with the Father. How can we experience something in the Spirit that the Lord did not enjoy, seeing that He has pre-eminence in all things?

First Manifestations

The first mention of the Spirit of God is in the second verse of Genesis chapter one. Thereafter, we see Him at work throughout the Law and the Prophets. However, in God's dealings with the Jews in those days, no one was filled with the Holy Spirit and nobody spoke in tongues. The Spirit only came upon the prophet, the priest and the king, and that only from time to time. The Spirit also anointed a few individuals for special tasks. An example of the Spirit of God coming upon someone is when the Spirit came upon Zechariah the priest.

---

2 CHRONICLES 24:20 – *Then the Spirit of God came upon Zechariah, the son of Jehoiada the priest, who stood above the people, and said to*

them, 'Thus says God: "Why do you transgress the commandments of the Lord, so that you cannot prosper?" Because you have forsaken the Lord, He also has forsaken you.'

God's intention to pour His Spirit on all (believing) people was made by a definite promise through the prophet Joel (Joel 2:28-29). No more would it only be the priest, the king and the prophet who would have the Spirit coming upon them, but every believer would have the privilege of the Spirit of the living God, dwelling in and operating through them. This prophecy was fulfilled, on the Day of Pentecost, fifty days after the Lord Jesus Christ rose from the dead.

ACTS 2:1-4 – *When the Day of Pentecost had fully come, they were all with one accord in one place. And suddenly there came a sound from heaven, as of a rushing mighty wind, and it filled the whole house where they were sitting. Then there appeared to them divided tongues, as of fire, and one sat upon each of them. And they were all filled with the Holy Spirit and began to speak with other tongues, as the Spirit gave them utterance.*

This was the first time that any believer got filled with the Holy Spirit and spoke in tongues. On that day, those newly Spirit-baptized believers found themselves spilling over into the street. They continued to speak in tongues and the strange happening of people speaking in other tongues began to attract a large crowd. Many of those who gathered were religious Jews from foreign countries, who had come to Jerusalem to worship. What totally amazed them was that they could understand, in their own languages, what these Holy Spirit-filled believers were saying in tongues.

They then began to enquire how this was possible and what this was all about. Peter pointed them to Joel's prophecy, saying, 'But this is what was spoken by the prophet Joel,' and then he preached Christ to them. More than three thousand people got saved that day. We can also reasonably assume that these new believers were also baptized in the Holy Spirit, and that they also spoke in tongues. Why? Peter himself had just assured them that the promise of the Baptism in the Holy Spirit and what they had witnessed was for them too (Acts 2:16). This is how the whole matter of the Baptism in the Holy Spirit and speaking in other tongues began.

There is no doubt that, as the gospel spread and more and more people believed in the Lord Jesus Christ, they too were led into being filled with the Holy Spirit. Out of what must have been thousands upon thousands of instances of people getting filled with the Holy Spirit in the days of the Book of Acts, four records are left for us to study.

A few years after the first outpouring of the Holy Spirit, there arose a great persecution against the church. Believers were scattered throughout the region. During this time Phillip went down to Samaria to preach the gospel there. A great many believed and were filled with joy. However, none of them were filled with the Holy Spirit. When the apostles who were at Jerusalem heard of the move of God that was taking place in Samaria, and that these new believers were not yet filled with the Spirit, they sent Peter and John to lay hands on them so that they could receive. This they did and the believers there received (Acts 8:14-17). Although the word tongues is not specifically mentioned, there is sufficient evidence that they did speak in tongues.

Then, during this great persecution of the Christians, Saul – who was later called Paul – made his way to Damascus, where he intended to further decimate the church. On his way there, the Lord appeared to him and he got saved. Temporarily blinded, he was led into Damascus to the home of a certain man called Judas. When he got there, there was nothing that he could do but pray. While he was praying, the Lord sent a devout man named Ananias to go and lay hands on him, so that he might receive the Holy Spirit. Ananias obeyed the Lord and Saul must have received (Acts 9:17).

The third record is found in the tenth chapter of the Book of Acts. Here, we are told how Cornelius and his household got saved and were filled with the Holy Spirit. The Lord dealt with Peter and his prejudices, and then sent him to preach the gospel to Cornelius and those of his household. Peter, accompanied by a few men, went to Caesarea, where Cornelius lived, and preached the gospel in his home. While Peter was preaching, the Holy Spirit fell on all those who believed, and they began to speak in tongues. Peter and his entourage were amazed but were convinced that these people had received the baptism in the Holy Spirit (Acts 10:44-48).

Paul, in his preaching in Greece, came to Ephesus and met some men there. They seemed to be disciples of John the Baptist. Paul preached the gospel to them, they believed and then he laid hands on them and they got filled with the Holy Spirit and spoke in tongues (Acts 19:1-7).

The Book of Acts establishes the fact that the Baptism in the Holy Spirit, with the evidence of speaking in other tongues, only began after the ascension of the Lord Jesus Christ. Before that, believers were not filled with the Holy Spirit and none spoke in tongues.

Out of these five records and other related scriptures in the epistles we will base our study and answer many questions that trouble the minds of people. The reader should not regard our deep digging into scripture as unnecessary repetition.

2 UNDERSTANDING TONGUES

Its Beginning is in the Baptism in the Holy Spirit

The first time someone speaks in tongues is when they get baptised in the Holy Spirit. It happens like this. When the person receives his or her salvation, the Holy Spirit causes the person's spirit to be born again. When He does that, He takes up residence in that person's spirit, albeit in the salvation dimension only.

ROMANS 8:9 – *But you are not in the flesh but in the Spirit, if indeed the Spirit of God dwells in you. Now if anyone does not have the Spirit of Christ, he is not His.*

The Lord Jesus Christ described this born-again experience as a fountain of water springing up into everlasting life. He also invited those who would believe in Him to be baptized in the Holy Spirit. This He described as rivers of living waters.

When a believer receives the Baptism in the Holy Spirit, the Spirit who is already in the person's spirit rises up and overwhelms the person.

At that moment, unknown words begin to sweep up from deep inside. The Spirit of God then loosens the dumb tongue of the person's spirit, giving him or her freedom to speak those words out. As the person yields, a jet of words is liberated from the person's spirit as they enjoy the fullness of the Holy Spirit. The born-again spirit of the person finds expression for the first time as the person speaks out in tongues.

Scriptural Evidence

The scriptural evidence of the Baptism in the Holy Spirit is speaking tongues. The scriptures are clear, and a simple study of the Book of Acts will prove that this is true. The Word of God is the believer's guide and the opinions of men must not influence us at all. We must hold fast to the truth, especially in these days when preachers are abandoning the clear teaching of the scriptures in this regard.

---

2 TIMOTHY 3:16-17 – *All Scripture is given by inspiration of God, and is profitable for doctrine, for reproof, for correction, for instruction in righteousness, that the man of God may be complete, thoroughly equipped for every good work.*

At the first instance of the Baptism in the Holy Spirit, on the Day of Pentecost, those who were filled with the Spirit of God spoke in tongues. This was the initial evidence that they were filled. The record is there for us to know what happened.

ACTS 2:1-4 – *When the Day of Pentecost had fully come, they were all with one accord in one place. And suddenly there came a sound from heaven, as of a rushing mighty wind, and it filled the whole house where they were sitting. Then there appeared to them divided tongues, as of fire, and one sat upon each of them. And they were all filled with the Holy Spirit and began to speak with other tongues, as the Spirit gave them utterance.*

The portion of scripture that tells us how Cornelius and his household got filled with the Holy Spirit proves beyond any doubt that speaking in tongues is the initial evidence of the baptism in the Holy Spirit (Acts 10:48). What convinced Peter and his entourage that these people (who must have believed the gospel while Peter was preaching) had been baptized in the Holy Spirit was the fact that they heard them speak in tongues. Peter's exact words were, 'Can anyone forbid water, that these should not be baptized who have received the Holy Spirit just as we have?' It cannot be any clearer. Their speaking in tongues was the proof that they had received the baptism in the Holy Spirit. The magnifying of God, in the simple gift of prophecy, followed.

The instance of Paul laying his hands on the believers in Ephesus also proves that speaking in tongues is the scriptural evidence of the baptism in the Holy Spirit. After Paul questioned these believers and discovered that they were not accurately instructed, he corrected their thinking and then laid his hands on them so that they could be baptized in the Holy Spirit. When he did that, they received and spoke in tongues. This is what convinced him that they had received. Their prophesying was a further manifestation of the Holy Spirit that followed the initial scriptural evidence (Acts 19:1-7).

The other two records of believers getting filled with the Holy Spirit do not specifically say that they spoke in tongues. However, by inference we know that they did. The one is in Samaria where the new believers received the baptism in the Holy Spirit (Acts 8:14-17) and the other one is of Paul receiving the Holy Spirit (Acts 9:17).

When Peter and John laid hands on the believers in Samaria to be filled with the Holy Spirit, Simon the Sorcerer observed the supernatural in manifestation. He wanted the same power to lay hands on people so that they could be filled with the Holy Spirit. Something must have registered on his senses. The inference that he heard them utter something comes from Peter's words. He said, "You have neither part nor portion in this matter, for your heart is not right in the sight of God." The Greek word that is rendered *matter* in the English translation is more accurately translated as utterance (Vine's: matter). It is therefore reasonable to conclude that these utterances were tongues. This was the sign that always convinced the apostles that someone had received the baptism in the Holy Spirit.

The record of the fact that Paul got filled with the Holy Spirit is given to us in the ninth chapter of the Book of Acts. We are not specifically told that Paul spoke in tongues when he got filled with the Spirit. However, we know that he did speak in tongues in his prayer life. In the bible days, no one laid hands on someone else to be filled with the Spirit and then sent them away, saying, "We will see the evidence that you have received the infilling of the Holy Spirit in your life by your greater enthusiasm for the gospel". When people spoke in tongues it was known that they had received the baptism in the Holy Spirit. It is also reasonable to conclude that Ananias laid hands on Paul, heard him speak in tongues and was satisfied that he had received the baptism in the Holy Spirit.

The fact that someone lifts up his or her voice, and supposedly prophesies is not proof that they are filled with the Holy Spirit. Nobody can exercise the gift of prophecy before being filled with the Holy Spirit, with the initial evidence of speaking in other tongues. Those who teach that prophesying can be proof of having been baptized in the Spirit are really trying to sidestep the need for receiving the baptism in the Holy Spirit with the supernatural evidence of speaking in tongues.

Falling under the power, shaking, running, jumping, screaming, shouting, dancing or any such, is not evidence that someone is filled with the Holy Spirit. The evidence is speaking in tongues. Being filled with joy after getting saved is not proof that one has been baptized in the Holy Spirit. In Samaria, where Phillip went to preach the gospel, the people believed and got saved, healed and delivered. As a result, they were filled with joy. However, they were only filled with the Holy Spirit when Peter and John came down from Jerusalem and laid hands on them. Joy is great, but it is only evidence of salvation, healing, deliverance and the like.

Preaching with great fervour, after 'receiving the Spirit', is not evidence that one has been baptized in the Holy Spirit. This only means that the preacher is adding more vim to the preaching. The preaching of a person who has received the baptism in the Holy Spirit, with the evidence of speaking in other tongues, is on a completely different and higher level.

If the Book of Acts is our guide, then we must accept that the only scriptural evidence for the baptism in the Holy Spirit is speaking in tongues and we must therefore reject all other opinions of men.

Tongues: What it is

There are nine gifts of the Holy Spirit. Paul lists them in the twelfth chapter of his first letter to the Corinthians.

---

1 Corinthians 12:8-11 – *for to one is given the word of wisdom through the Spirit, to another the word of knowledge through the same Spirit, to another faith by the same Spirit, to another gifts of healings by the same Spirit, to another the working of miracles, to another prophecy, to another discerning of spirits, to another different kinds of tongues, to another the interpretation of tongues.*

Different Kinds of Tongues is one of the gifts. In the New King James version of the bible the word *different* is in italics. This means that the word is not in the original writing but has been supplied by the translators, to give greater sense to the phrase. The word 'kinds' is in the plural and indicates variety, so the word different is a good addition. In the Old King James Version of the bible, the gift is called 'Divers Kinds of Tongues'. Divers is an old English word for different. The gift is therefore accurately called Different Kinds of Tongues. What follows is the definition of the gift.

Different Kinds of Tongues are Holy Spirit-given utterances, through a Spirit-filled believer, that constitute languages never learned, nor understood, by the speaker and, in nearly all occurrences, not understood by the hearer.

Different Kinds of Tongues is a gift of utterance. It is also referred to as a vocal gift or a gift of inspiration. The other two gifts of utterance are Prophecy and Interpretation of Tongues.

When a Spirit-filled believer speaks in tongues, it is the mind of the Spirit of God that is expressed. The Spirit uses the yielded speech organs of the Spirit-filled believer and gives that person supernatural utterances in a language that has never been learned by that speaker. No human thoughts can therefore contaminate the divine utterances.

Speaking in tongues is a manifestation of a vocal miracle every time one yields to the Spirit. There is absolutely nothing natural about tongues. It is not a learned language.

Tongues are sounds that constitute languages, although the sounds may sound unintelligible to hearers. Notwithstanding the fact that they are described as gibberish by unlearned hearers, every word has deep significance. Paul deals thoroughly with this in his first letter to the Corinthians. Unfortunately, the full force of his words is lost because of a poor translation.

---

1 CORINTHIANS 14:10 – *There are, it may be, so many kinds of languages in the world, and none of them is without significance.*

The English word 'languages' is a translation of the Greek word 'phone' and the meaning of this Greek word is 'a sound' (Vine's: Voice/Sound). Languages is a very poor translation. The fact that the English word 'phonics' is derived from the Greek word 'phone' proves that 'sound' is the correct translation of the word. Phone relates to articulated sounds. Paul's words should rather be read as, 'There are, it may be, so many kinds of articulated sounds in the world, and none of them are without significance'.

It is clear that Paul is saying that tongues is not gibberish because articulated sounds used in communication, although not understood by the hearer, have meaning. These sounds grouped together constitute languages and have meaning to those who understand them. We all have heard people from remote tribes speak a language that sounds like total gibberish, but we know that these seemingly unintelligible sounds are a rich language that is understood by other members of the tribe.

Even communication among animals of the same species must have significance. The sounds that these animals make seem to be senseless sounds to us. However, this does not mean that they have no meaning. The cow makes one loud 'moo' and all the other cows understand and follow. What they understood was, 'It is time to head home'. A mother hen gives a certain cluck and all her chicks joyfully follow her and start pecking at the ground as they feed. At another time, a sentry bird gives a loud shriek, and the mother hen interprets the meaning to be, 'There is a hawk circling above,' and gives another series of clucks and all the chicks scurry behind her as she hurries for shelter. What they understood was, 'Follow me, hurry, the hawk is about to swoop on us'. Another cluck and all the chicks understand, 'Under my feathers and hide!' The lion, the tiger, the whale, the eagle, the mouse, all make sounds communicating with one another.

Likewise, tongues, may sound like gibberish, but they are not. Demons know that and come out screaming when this so-called gibberish is spoken. Visions are manifest when this so-called gibberish is spoken. Tongues are sounds that constitute rich languages.

The nature of tongues is also a surprise to many. From heaven's point of view, they are treated as a tangible substance that is collected in spiritual vessels and released before the Father (Rev. 5:8).

Speaking Directly and Perfectly to God

A Spirit-filled believer who speaks in tongues speaks directly and perfectly to God. It is a hotline to heaven. The devil does not know what the Spirit-filled believer is praying about. He only feels the reverberations in the spirit world and experiences the ramifications of such kind of praying. This is the Lord's shocking surprise for the enemy who never dreamt of a day that would come where he would not know a thing of what someone was praying about. Now, who can top that?

---

1 CORINTHIANS 14:2 – *For he who speaks in a tongue does not speak to men but to God, for no one understands him; however, in the spirit he speaks mysteries.*

When a believer prays in the understanding, his or her limited knowledge and intellect comes to bear on the prayer. Such kind of praying always falls far below the glory of God. Our shortcoming is that we do not know what to pray for as we should. It is therefore impossible to pray perfect prayers in our natural learned language.

ROMANS 8:26-27 – *Likewise the Spirit also helps in our weaknesses. For we do not know what we should pray for as we ought, but the Spirit Himself makes intercession for us with groanings which cannot be uttered. Now He who searches the hearts knows what the mind of the Spirit is, because He makes intercession for the saints according to the will of God.*

All believers get to a place where they stand mute, wanting to express thanksgiving, praise, worship, love or adoration to the Father. At these times, when human abilities fail the believer, tongues come to the rescue. Tongues perfectly express the deepest desires of our spirit.

Definition: Praying in the Spirit

Praying in the Spirit is praying in tongues. There are three scriptures in the Epistles that prove that this is true. The first one is in Jude's letter. In it he exhorts believers to pray in the Holy Spirit.

JUDE 1:20 – *But you, beloved, building yourselves up on your most holy faith, praying in the Holy Spirit.*

Paul also instructed the Ephesians to pray 'in the Spirit'. This is the same terminology that Jude used. This tells us that, across the church world at that time, believers understood exactly what praying in the Spirit was.

EPHESIANS 6:18 – *praying always with all prayer and supplication in the Spirit, being watchful to this end with all perseverance and supplication for all the saints.*

The second verse of the fourteenth chapter of Paul's first letter to the Corinthian church defines exactly what praying in the Spirit is. Paul wrote, "For he who speaks in a tongue, does not speak to men but to God, for no one understands him; however, in the Spirit he speaks mysteries." According to this scripture, speaking in tongues is speaking in the Spirit. This is what the believers understood when they read Jude's letter and what Paul meant in his letter to the Ephesians.

Praying faster and with liberty in a learned language is not praying in the Spirit. Strengthening muscles and praying out fervently is not praying in the Spirit. Shaking the body, shouting out loudly, swinging arms and shouting hallelujah over and over again is not praying in the Holy Spirit. Reacting with goose bumps and shivering and shaking is not praying in the Holy Spirit. Kneeling down very quietly, and lifting up hands to heaven and saying, "Good morning, Holy Spirit," is not praying in the Spirit. Putting a holy look on one's face is not praying in the Holy Spirit. Blowing breath out of the mouth and saying, "Holy Spirit, fill up this room," is not praying in the Spirit.

Although it is true that praying in the Spirit is praying in tongues, sometimes a prayer will emerge out of the spirit of the tongue-talking believer in a known language. This could either be a manifestation of the gift of Interpretation of Tongues or the simple gift of Prophecy. Both of these manifestations will be speaking in the Spirit, but the speaking in tongues always comes first. One cannot decide to speak in the Spirit in a known language as one decides to speak in tongues. Those who interpret tongues and prophesy must first be full of the Spirit, having prayed at length in tongues in their private prayer life.

The Spirit of Man Prays

When a believer is baptized in the Holy Spirit, that person will speak in tongues. At that moment, the person's spirit is liberated, the spirit tongue is loosed, and the person speaks in tongues.

ACTS 2:4 – *And they were all filled with the Holy Spirit and began to speak with other tongues, as the Spirit gave them utterance.*

After the person is baptized in the Holy Spirit, if taught correctly he or she will embark on a life of praying in tongues. Understanding what is happening when a person is praying in tongues becomes important. Some people think that the Holy Spirit does the praying through the believer. This is not the case at all. The explanation given below will be helpful in understanding this.

Man is a spirit; he has a soul and lives in a body. The spirit is the real person and is described in the bible as the inner man. The soul is made up of the emotions, the mind, the intelligence and the thought patterns of the person. The body is the physical part.

When a person prays in his or her learned language, it is the soul that is praying because the person who is praying understands the words that are being spoken out. When a Spirit-filled believer prays in tongues, it is the spirit of the person that prays. The Holy Spirit helps, but it is the person's spirit that prays. Paul made a clear statement in this regard.

I Corinthians 14:14 – *For if I pray in a tongue, my spirit prays, but my understanding is unfruitful.*

It is the born-again spirit of a Spirit-filled believer that is active when he or she is praying in tongues. The human mind is quiescent. Tongues are not words coming from the person's mind and none of the thought patterns of the person's natural mind can interfere with this divine exercise.

While the person is praying in tongues, the spirit of the person with Holy Spirit utterances expresses the omnipotent thoughts of God. It can edify itself, refresh itself, rest itself, worship, pray out the divine plan and purpose and access all the capabilities of God. The spirit of man desires and has a great need to pray.

Think about this. If the person does not pray in tongues, that person's spirit does not pray. This means that the real person never prays. Now, that is a sad state of affairs; that is, the real person never praying, never speaking, never edifying itself, never worshipping and never doing anything that goes with praying in tongues. Although the person may pray much in the understanding, it still remains a very, very, very sad state of affairs.

God has provided a means whereby the born-again spirit can pray apart from the natural mind, and access all His glory. Sadly, the believer denies his or her spirit the right and privilege of being actively involved in the downloading of the blessings of God. They stick with the lowly praying in the understanding.

Not a Minor Gift

Tongues is not a minor gift. There is no scripture in the bible that tells us that this gift is any less than any of the others. Those who say so are only giving a conclusion that they arrived at themselves.

All the gifts of the Holy Spirit were manifested under the Old Covenant, except Different Kinds of Tongues and Interpretation of Tongues. These two gifts were reserved for those who would be born again. They were given under the better New Covenant that has been established upon far better promises. There must be something about tongues that makes it far better than the other gifts.

HEBREWS 8:6 – *But now He has obtained a more excellent ministry, inasmuch as He is also Mediator of a better covenant, which was established on better promises.*

Tongues is a powerful gift of the Spirit. Every word spoken in tongues is a direct utterance of the divine mind and it brings tremendous power on the scene. Every word that proceeds out of the mouth of God is more explosive then a trillion nuclear explosions put together.

LUKE 1:37 – *For with God nothing is ever impossible and no word from God shall be without power or impossible of fulfilment. (Amplified)*

When a Spirit-filled believer prays in tongues, that person is not activating some teeny-weeny spirit but the almighty Spirit of the living God. In the spirit world, there are awesome ramifications and reverberations that blast demonic forces out of the way. The demonic world knows all about the power of a person who speaks in tongues. Great and mighty is the Spirit of the Lord. He is the Greater One (1 John 4:4).

The Holy Spirit knows ahead of time of the planned activities of the devil and his cohorts. Sometimes, they intend coming in with a huge assault against the believer. When this impending attack approaches, He will urge the Spirit-filled believer to engage in a long, solid session of praying in tongues. If the believer yields, then the Greater One raises up a standard against devil that brings him to a halt (Is. 59:19). The breath of the Lord drives a rushing stream of power against the ominous approach of the wicked and his attack dissipates into nothing. Tongues is the breath of the Lord.

If this were a minor gift, why would Paul be grateful that he spoke in tongues more than the entire church at Corinth? (1 Cor. 14:18). Paul, a prolific speaker in tongues, knew the great value of tongues, and practised it in his daily life.

The Plurality of the Gift

The name Different Kinds of Tongues immediately gives an indication that there is a plurality in the gift. Studying the scriptures, one will readily see that there are different kinds, different levels, different purposes and different uses of tongues.

---

1 CORINTHIANS 12:10 – *... to another different kinds of tongues...*

First, there is a tongue that the believer speaks in when he or she gets baptized in the Holy Spirit. Many people who get baptized in the Holy Spirit will testify that they spoke in a certain type of tongue at that moment and never spoke in that tongue again.

Second, there is a tongue that a believer speaks in his or her private devotions. These are usually called devotional tongues. It does not need an initial anointing to get started. The Spirit-filled believer can speak in tongues whenever he or she wants to. He or she just begins and yields to the Holy Spirit and prays in tongues.

Third, on this devotional level each believer has a different tongue that they speak in. There are therefore millions of different tongues that rise up to God as Spirit-filled believers yield to the Holy Spirit.

Fourth, when a believer is praying in his or her usual devotional tongues, sometimes a new, fresh tongue and maybe another that the person is not accustomed to speaking in, is given. The believer is truly speaking in tongues.

Fifth, the Holy Spirit sometimes pulls the person who is praying in tongues into even deeper praying in tongues, called groaning. These are tongues that cannot be articulated normally (Rom. 8:26-28).

Sixth, some people have a public gift of speaking in tongues (1 Cor. 14:27). When in a gathering of believers, those who are used in this way might sense the anointing to speak out in tongues. When this happens, the person, normally known by the group of believers, will lift up his or her voice as a hush comes on the congregation, and will speak out aloud in tongues. That person or another will then give the interpretation. This level of speaking in tongues has a greater anointing than devotional tongues.

Seventh, sometimes in the public use of the gift a person will unknowingly speak in a language never learned, but one that is known by someone in the congregation. This convinces the person that what was said in tongues is divine. God sometimes astounds this person further when He uses someone else to give a perfect interpretation. Now who can top that? I ask again: Now, who in the big whole wide world can top that?

Eighth, there is what is called a Ministry Gift of Tongues (1 Cor. 12:28-30). This is not just a public gift of speaking in tongues but a definite ministry gift with a heavier anointing. People who have this gift will speak in tongues and then interpret what was said in tongues, giving the recipient divine direction. Sometimes it might be two people operating in the gift, for example a husband and wife. A person might be called out of a crowd and one of the spouses speaks in tongues over the person and the other gives the interpretation. This could continue over several different people. People get ministered to individually and leave the gathering knowing that they received a word from the Lord.

MARK 16:17 – *In My name they... will speak with new tongues.*

By the Will of Man

Speaking in tongues is an exercise of the will of the Spirit-baptized believer. The onus does not lie on the Holy Spirit. Although, it is 'as the Spirit wills' that a person speaks in tongues in a public assembly of believers, it is still the believer who must exercise his or her will and speak out in the unknown language. Praying and speaking in tongues is the believer's responsibility.

---

1 CORINTHIANS 14:15 – *What is the conclusion then? I will pray with the spirit, and I will also pray with the understanding. I will sing with the spirit, and I will also sing with the understanding.*

The scripture given above makes it clear that Paul willed to pray in the Spirit and willed to sing in the Spirit. He was the one who decided to do so and not the Holy Spirit. He did it.

The fact that God has placed regulations on the use of the gift in a public assembly of believers proves that the restraint and the operation of the gift is within the power of the believer. In a public assembly, no more than three Spirit-filled believers are at liberty to speak out loud in tongues (1 Cor. 14:27-29). The rest of the believers who are present are to exercise their will and not speak out aloud in tongues, even if they sense an anointing.

---

1 CORINTHIANS 14:16 – *And the spirits of the prophets are subject to the prophets.*

The fact that the believer is instructed to stir up the gift that is resident in him or her also proves that the believer has the ability to do so (2 Tim. 1:6).

It is up to the believer to make a decision to speak in tongues. When going to prayer, the believer decides to pray in tongues and then goes ahead and speaks. This can be done even if the believer feels as dry as a bone and has no feeling of the presence of the Holy Spirit at all. It is as simple as that.

Those who teach that a Spirit-baptized believer should wait for some sort of feeling of ecstasy or anointing before embarking on praying or speaking in tongues, rob God's people of a lifetime of blessings. Such feelings might never come. Believers will find themselves waiting for years upon years with no such feelings ever arriving. Sadly, they eventually die, having missed the joy of speaking in tongues and all the resultant benefits that could have been theirs.

The Lord Jesus Christ Himself gave every believer the right and privilege to speak in tongues when He said, "In My name they shall speak in tongues". Who then has the right to forbid them to do so when we are further instructed not to forbid believers from speaking in tongues? (1 Cor. 14:39)

After getting baptized in the Holy Spirit, with the initial evidence of speaking in tongues, believers should not stop there but should go on and enjoy a lifetime of speaking in tongues and reap all the benefits that go with it.

Gateway to Supernatural

Different Kinds of Tongues is the gateway to the supernatural. It is the arrival 'city' that gives entrance into the land of milk and honey. It is first tongues and then the other gifts. Anointing and deeper anointing, revelation knowledge, guidance, prosperity, healing, deliverance and the host of other blessings that flow from the hand of God come afterwards.

The gospel era was begun with the apostles being baptized in the Holy Spirit. This baptism was accompanied by speaking in tongues. Speaking in tongues came first and then the miraculous that became commonplace in their lives.

ACTS 2:1-2 – *When the Day of Pentecost had fully come, they were all with one accord in one place. And suddenly there came a sound from heaven, as of a rushing mighty wind, and it filled the whole house where they were sitting. Then there appeared to them divided tongues, as of fire, and one sat upon each of them. And they were all filled with the Holy Spirit and began to speak with other tongues, as the Spirit gave them utterance.*

This principle is further demonstrated in other baptisms in the Holy Spirit that are recorded in the Book of Acts. It was always tongues first, and then prophecy, and not the other way around. At Cornelius' home, when his believing family were baptized in the Holy Spirit, they first spoke in tongues and then they magnified God. The magnifying God in the natural language was the prophesying part that followed. Likewise, the Ephesian believers who got filled with the Holy Spirit in Acts, chapter nineteen, first spoke in tongues and then they prophesied.

ACTS 10:46...19:6 – *For they heard them speak with tongues and magnify God... And when Paul had laid hands on them, the Holy Spirit came upon them, and they spoke with tongues and prophesied.*

Tongues precedes the gift of Interpretation of Tongues. This is an obvious truth, but it is still true that tongues come first and the other follows. When tongues are completed with interpretation, it is equivalent to prophecy. So once again it is tongues first and then prophecy.

Those who pray at length in tongues position themselves for the manifestation of Interpretation of Tongues, Prophecy, the Word of Wisdom, the Word of Knowledge, Discerning of Spirits, Special Faith, the Gifts of Healings and the Working of Miracles (1 Cor. 12:8-10). Tongues is the gateway to the other gifts of the Spirit.

Those who have been called to one of the ministry gifts of Apostle, Prophet, Evangelist, Pastor or Teacher, will find a deeper anointing developing in their lives as they pray at length in tongues. It is tongues that brings the greater supernatural weight of the ministry gift into manifestation. The same applies to all other dimensions of the workings of God. Believers must always remember that the gateway to the supernatural is tongues.

Interpretation of Tongues

One of the nine gifts of the Holy Spirit is Interpretation of Tongues. This book is about speaking in tongues, so a brief study of this closely-related gift, Interpretation of Tongues, will be helpful. This teaching is not an attempt at an exhaustive study of the subject at all. It is merely one that will give the speaker in tongues insight into the gift. Paul listed the nine gifts of the Holy Spirit in his letter to the Corinthians.

---

1 CORINTHIANS 12:8-10 – *for to one is given the word of wisdom through the Spirit, to another the word of knowledge through the same Spirit, to another faith by the same Spirit, to another gifts of healings by the same Spirit, to another the working of miracles, to another prophecy, to another discerning of spirits, to another different kinds of tongues, to another the interpretation of tongues.*

The gift of Interpretation of Tongues is one of the three vocal gifts. Different Kinds of Tongues and Prophecy are the other two. These gifts are referred as gifts of utterance, vocal gifts or gifts of inspiration. The definition of the gift given below must be studied closely because all that the gift is, is captured in a succinct statement.

Interpretation of Tongues are Holy Spirit-given words in a known language, through a Spirit-filled believer, that sets out the meaning of that which has been spoken in tongues.

This truth is brought out in Paul's instructions to the Corinthian church. He made it clear that tongues without the meaning of it, would be speaking in the air.

---

1 CORINTHIANS 14:11 – *Therefore, if I do not know the meaning of the language, I shall be a foreigner to him who speaks, and he who speaks will be a foreigner to me.*

The Spirit-filled believer who interprets tongues does not translate that which was spoken in tongues into a known language. It is not a word-for-word translation. The gift is not called Translation of Tongues but Interpretation of Tongues. This is why, when a long message in tongues is given, only a short interpretation sometimes follows. At other times, a short message in tongues is followed by a long interpretation. The reason for this is that the person used in the gift of Interpretation of Tongues only shows forth the meaning of that which was spoken in tongues. Notwithstanding this, the Lord does sometimes use a Spirit-filled believer to translate tongues word for word. This happens in special cases.

Interpretation of tongues is not a repetition of portions of scripture because this would be speaking from human memory, whereas interpretation of tongues come from the mind of God. The mind of a believer plays no part in Interpretation of Tongues. Just as the speaking in tongues is purely an expression of the mind of God, so is the interpretation of tongues. It is all the mind of God.

Those who interpret tongues do not understand what was spoken in tongues. They pay no attention to the words of the message that is given in tongues. Instead, they rest purely on faith that the Holy Spirit will use them to give an accurate interpretation. After the message of tongues has been spoken out aloud, they look to God and under the anointing speak boldly, giving an interpretation.

The gift of Interpretation of Tongues is a supernatural manifestation of the Holy Spirit. There is absolutely nothing natural about it. Its manifestation is always a glorious miracle. Every attempt to reduce it to the natural, is error. Some wishing to sidestep the supernatural nature of Interpretation of Tongues call it the Gift of Interpretation.

These people who teach that this so-called 'Gift of Interpretation' exists, hold that it gives the person who has it a sharp sense of understanding of the scriptures and the ability to explain its meaning more easily than others. Such a gift does not exist and the advocacy, and supposed practice of it, is ludicrous. A keen understanding of the scriptures comes from the spirit of wisdom and revelation that all Spirit-filled believers can benefit from when they speak at length in tongues.

The purpose of the gift is to give intelligent understanding of that which was spoken in tongues, so that the hearers may be edified. Sometimes, the Spirit will bring the gift of Interpretation of Tongues into manifestation when a person is privately praying in tongues. This is to give that person understanding of a portion of his or her praying in tongues. This is for more direct leading. Spirit-filled believers are therefore encouraged to pray that the gift of Interpretation of Tongues operate in their lives (1 Cor. 14:13).

Different Kinds of Tongues and Interpretation of Tongues must not be viewed as lowly gifts. Seven of the nine gifts of the Spirit were manifested under the Law and the Prophets. However, the gifts of Different Kinds of Tongues and Interpretation of Tongues only began to manifest under the New Covenant. Although they may appear as insignificant gifts to some, their awesomeness is amplified by the fact that they were reserved for a new and better covenant, established upon better promises (Heb. 8:6).

3 GOVERNANCE

Public Speaking in Tongues

Although it is the Lord's will that the gift of Different Kind of Tongues be used for edification in a believer's gathering and has given the believer the ability to use the gift, He has not given them carte blanche. There are regulations that govern the use of the gift.

---

1 CORINTHIANS 14:40 – *Let all things be done decently and in order.*

A stranger should be stopped if he or she suddenly stands up in a gathering of believers and speaks out aloud in tongues with the purpose of ministering to them. The leader of the gathering would be perfectly within his or her rights and responsibility to stop that person from ministering because the group would not have had opportunity to judge the fruits of that person (Matt. 7:15-20).

Nobody should get up in a believers' meeting while someone else is speaking in tongues, prophesying, singing, preaching or teaching the Word and lift up their voice and proceed to speak in tongues. If another, and then several others, did the same thing, then the speaker and the rest of the congregation would be even more bewildered.

People who do so are obviously ignoring the fact that God is using someone else at that time. By doing this they introduce man-made confusion and the devil, who is in the business of confusion, takes advantage of the situation. Some people who are present in such a gathering might never come back again. All believers must remember that God is a God of order and that they must not interrupt someone else who already has the floor.

---

1 CORINTHIANS 14:27-33 – *If anyone speaks in a tongue, let there be two or at the most three, each in turn, and let one interpret. But if there is no interpreter, let him keep silent in church, and let him speak to himself and to God. Let two or three prophets speak, and let the others judge. But if anything is revealed to another who sits by, let the first keep silent. For you can all prophesy one by one, that all may learn, and all may be encouraged. And the spirits of the prophets are subject to the prophets. For God is not the author of confusion but of peace, as in all the churches of the saints.*

A Spirit-filled believer who is used by God in public speaking in tongues should not get up in a gathering of believers and lift up his or her voice, speak out aloud in tongues and then just sit down leaving the tongues uninterpreted. That would be of no benefit to the assembly of believers at all. This person would just be speaking into the air.

Believers who yield in this manner, must first of all be prepared to interpret the tongues that they speak out themselves. If the person does not feel confident in interpreting the tongues, then that person must not speak out aloud. He or she need not be concerned that they are disobeying God because it is written 'the spirit of the prophet is subject to the prophet'.

It is always preferable that somebody else interprets the tongues that somebody speaks as public ministry. So a person who is about to speak in tongues must first ascertain that a person or persons are present who are used by God in the gift of Interpretation of Tongues before they speak. The believer who spoke in tongues must then give a few moments for one of these people to interpret and, if no one responds, then the speaker in tongues must proceed to interpret. If the believer is not used in interpretation and knows that no one present is, the person must not deliver the public message. The person should release the pent-up pressure of the Spirit by speaking softly in tongues to himself or herself and to God. They should not even disturb the people sitting close by. This boils down to common sense, yet the Spirit condescends and gives an explanation so that there may be no confusion.

Paul used the strumming of a harp and the blowing of a flute or trumpet to show why tongues spoken as a public message to an assembly of believers should be interpreted (1 Cor. 14:7-8). Blowing a flute or strumming a harp with uncertain sounds will not get anybody to sing along. However, if the hearers recognize a tune, they could interpret the meaning and then they could sing together in unison.

If a trumpet was blown in the midst of an army with no certain message, soldiers would not know how to respond. However, if a familiar sound that meant 'start marching' was blown, then the soldiers would respond. Likewise, if somebody speaks in tongues and there is no interpretation, then nobody can respond to the unknown words.

Where the Spirit is moving and people realize that they have a message to deliver in tongues, they should, in addition to having made sure beforehand that the message in tongues can be interpreted, call to remembrance that, at most, only three Spirit-filled believers should speak. Each person wanting to speak in tongues should wait for his or her turn before speaking. One person should not give three fragments of a message and consider that as three. Only one person should interpret a message. Two people must not compete in interpreting the same message. When the second message is given, then the same person who interpreted the first message or another person may interpret, and so with the third.

If a fourth person attempts to speak in tongues, that person should be stopped and after the service corrected. It would be considered total madness if people all over the congregation began to lift up their voices trying to deliver public messages in tongues.

When they want to give a public message in tongues, believers should also be conscious of the presence of unbelievers and those who are not taught in the things of the Spirit. For example, if the president of the country visited the church and the believers started having a believers' meeting and spoke in tongues, with or without interpretation, this would not be fitting. The spirits of the prophets are subject to the prophets.

In every one of the cases given above, the person who speaks in tongues must know that they have control over their own spirit and over the manifestation of the gift of speaking in tongues. They decide to yield or not to yield.

Nobody should forbid believers from speaking in tongues. Some ministers who are afraid to allow the Holy Spirit to move in case something goes wrong, try to suppress the gift. In an assembly where the Holy Spirit is given free sway, things will go wrong from time to time. Those in charge must just know that all things must be done decently and in order (1 Cor. 14:40).

A Sign

Although the gift of tongues is for the edification of a believer, for use in prayer and intercession, and for the public edification of believers (when accompanied with the gift of Interpretation of Tongues), it is also a sign to unbelievers. It is a sign that they sometimes reject, and a sign that they sometimes accept. It is also a sign to believers that God is in their midst.

Paul deals with the sign of tongues that unbelievers reject in his first letter to the Corinthians. A simple reading of this passage of scripture should quickly bring any honest student of the Word to the conclusion that tongues is a sign to unbelievers, but one that they reject.

---

1 CORINTHIANS 14:20-22 – *Brethren, do not be children in understanding; however, in malice be babes, but in understanding be mature. In the law it is written, "With men of other tongues and other lips I will speak to this people; and yet, for all that, they will not hear Me," says the Lord. Therefore, tongues are for a sign, not to those who believe but to unbelievers; but prophesying is not for unbelievers but for those who believe.*

Paul used the exact words that God used when declaring that the disobedient Jews of those days would not believe, even if an invading army came amongst them, speaking a foreign tongue. He used this passage of scripture to prove to the Corinthians that it was useless to use tongues to get unbelievers to repent. The full quotation from the Book of Isaiah is given below so that the reader can follow the argument Paul made.

ISAIAH 28:8-11 – *Whom will He teach knowledge? and whom will He make to understand the message? Those just weaned from milk? Those just drawn from the breasts? For precept must be upon precept, precept upon precept, line upon line, line upon line, Here a little, there a little." For with stammering lips and another tongue He will speak to this people, to whom He said, 'This is the rest with which You may cause the weary to rest,' And, 'This is the refreshing'; Yet they would not hear. But the word of the Lord was to them, 'Precept upon precept, precept upon precept, Line upon line, line upon line, here a little, there a little,' that they might go and fall backward, and be broken and snared and caught.*

Isaiah said that these disobedient Jews, who had slid into gross sin, were like babes who had just been drawn from the breasts of their mothers, were hard of hearing and had to be taught little by little. Even though they were dealt with like this, they would still not realize their need for repentance. As a result of them refusing to listen to the prophets, they would eventually be overcome by a foreign invasion. The invading nation would come among them, speaking in a foreign tongue. This would be a sign to them that prophecy was being fulfilled right in the midst of them. However, even this obvious sign that God was speaking to them, 'with stammering lips and another tongue', would be rejected by them and they would end up in captivity.

Paul used precisely the same argument that God used to prove that tongues, although a sign to unbelievers, would be rejected by them. Read the first quotation above and you will see that he first appealed to the Corinthians not to be spiritual babes, like the Jews of old, saying, "Brethren, do not be children in understanding; however, in malice be babes, but in understanding be mature".

Paul proved from scripture that, just as unknown tongues were ineffective and were rejected by disobedient Israel, so tongues would prove to be ineffective and be rejected by unbelievers in Corinth. Unbelievers in Corinth would no doubt hear about the speaking of tongues in the church that was in their city, and some would even have first-hand experience by walking into a believer's assembly. The hearing of people speaking in tongues would certainly be a sign to them but, like disobedient Israel, they would reject it.

Sometimes, tongues are also used in such a miraculous way that they become a sign that unbelievers cannot ignore. There are many testimonies of believers who were drawn out of sin into the saving grace of our Lord Jesus Christ through the manifestation of the Gifts of Tongues and Interpretation of Tongues. They tell of a day when they were present in an assembly of believers when miraculously someone spoke in tongues in a language that they understood and were even more astounded when someone else gave a perfect interpretation. There is no topping a demonstration of the Holy Spirit such as that.

On the Day of Pentecost, the apostles and those who were with them were filled with the Holy Spirit and began to speak in other tongues, as the Spirit gave them utterance. Visible tongues of fire rested on their heads and a sound like a mighty rushing wind was heard, not only by those getting filled, but by many in Jerusalem. Those who heard the sound rushed to where the upper room was and were greeted by an inexplicable miracle. These newly Spirit-filled believers were speaking in tongues, and those in the crowd understood what they were saying.

The miracle was not only that these uneducated Galileans were speaking in unknown tongues, but that each hearer understood what was being said in their own native language. This was an obvious supernatural sign. Some accepted the sign as one from God and heeded

Peter's preaching and got saved, while others simply rejected it (Acts 2:6-12).

Tongues are also a sign to believers that God is in their midst. The miraculous events described above, and just the very speaking of tongues for edification, strengthens the faith of Spirit-filled believers.

Prominence

Pentecostals and Charismatics are accused of giving prominence to this gift. This is not the case at all, although it might appear to be so to the uninformed. Spirit-filled believers really put emphasis on the salvation message and not tongues. They are always preaching that Jesus Christ is the only hope of salvation. Among those who are saved, the preaching of the gospel is the main message.

---

1 CORINTHIANS 2:2 – *For I determined not to know anything among you except Jesus Christ and Him crucified.*

This gift brings extraordinary interest from people from without. People respond as the Jews did on the day of Pentecost. Some are amazed and completely baffled when they hear people speak in tongues. Those who mock the manifestation must be counted in with all those who show interest in the gift. As a result of this, there is much discussion around this gift. This makes people think that we are giving prominence to the gift.

ACTS 2:12 – *So they were all amazed and perplexed, saying to one another, "Whatever could this mean?"*

Another reason why it appears that this gift is given prominence is because people in the church world, and even believers who are in circles where the Baptism in the Holy Spirit is believed, are always enquiring about the gift. Some of those who are uninformed want to debate the validity of the gift for today. Tongues becomes the issue to so many people. As a result of this, Spirit-filled believers find themselves regularly pressed to give an answer to these people (1 Peter 3:15).

Every time a person is baptized in the Holy Spirit, they always speak in tongues because this is the initial evidence of the baptism in the Holy Spirit (Acts 2:4; 10:48; 19:6). So, because of this indispensable manifestation, people think that tongues get undue attention.

There is always a need to spur Spirit-filled believers on to exercise the gift and to speak in tongues. The false notion that it's the Holy Spirit's responsibility to speak in tongues has to be broken down. Spirit-filled preachers faced with this ignorance find themselves obliged to teach on this gift more often than on the other gifts. When believers give heed to correct teaching and obey, they start yielding to the Spirit and speak in tongues. The uninformed observer thinks that prominence has being given to this gift.

Different Kinds of Tongues is a gift that every Spirit-filled believer has a right to exercise. The bible encourages all to speak in tongues (1 Cor. 14:5). So, the large majority of members in Spirit-filled circles speak in tongues. Different Kinds of Tongues is therefore a prolific gift.

In the church itself, where there is so much misunderstanding of the gift and careless exposition on this important subject, an accurate teaching of the gift becomes necessary. It is not just critics who need to be answered, but believers themselves have to be taught the details of the gift.

All the gifts of the Spirit are sought after in circles where the Holy Spirit is cherished. However, because this gift is the gateway to the supernatural, this is where everybody begins.

PART THREE

FALSE DOCTRINES

1 ERROR: THE GIFTS HAVE PASSED AWAY

Last Apostle Doctrine

Some teach that only the twelve Apostles of the Lamb were baptized in the Holy Spirit on the Day of Pentecost and because of this only they could pass this baptism on to others. So, when these apostles died, they say, there was nobody left who could pass the Baptism in the Holy Spirit on to new believers. According to them this means that all the gifts of the Holy Spirit, including the gift of Different Kinds of Tongues, ceased to manifest after the death of the last Apostle of the Lamb. This is a false doctrine. Obviously false, as all false doctrines are.

Peter, who was one of the Apostles of the Lamb, had no inkling of such doctrine. This is proven by the statement that he made on the Day of Pentecost. He preached that the Baptism in the Holy Spirit was for those before him, for the next generation and for all the generations who were yet to come. Now we ask, and wish, that this matter could be laid to rest right here and now. How could the generations who were still *afar off* receive the Baptism in the Holy Spirit, after all the Apostles of the Lamb had died, seeing that, according to the advocates of this doctrine, only they could lay hands on believers to be filled with the Spirit?

Acts 2:38-39 – *Then Peter said to them, 'Repent, and let every one of you be baptized in the name of Jesus Christ for the remission of sins; and you shall receive the gift of the Holy Spirit. For the promise is to you and to your children, and to all who are afar off, as many as the Lord our God will call.'*

To further expose this error, I point out that the bible does not say that only the twelve Apostles of the Lamb received the Baptism in the Holy Spirit on the Day of Pentecost. It can be reasonably assumed that there were others present when the Holy Spirit was poured out on that day.

The first chapter of the Book of Acts tells us that there were about a hundred and twenty disciples who had gathered in the Upper Room. Mary, the mother of Jesus, the Lord's brothers, other men and women were also there. These 'all continued with one accord in prayer and supplication' (Acts 1:14-15).

The divine record does not say that any of these people stopped waiting on the Lord to be endued with power from on High. Instead it says that, when the Day of Pentecost arrived, 'they were *all* with one accord in one place', and then 'they were *all* filled with the Holy Spirit and began to speak with other tongues, as the Spirit gave them utterance' (Acts 2:1-4). So, all those who were present got filled with the Spirit. The fact that Peter stood up with the eleven and began to preach does not mean that the others were not in the background.

However, if it is granted that only the twelve Apostles of the Lamb were filled with the Spirit on the Day of Pentecost, the scriptures still prove that the teaching being discussed is a false doctrine.

Why? The Baptism in the Holy Spirit does not get passed on to the next person. That's a wrong understanding of things regarding the Spirit. Every believer receives the Spirit when he or she gets born again, albeit only in the salvation dimension of the Spirit. When hands are laid on them to be filled with the Holy Spirit, the Spirit who is already within that person overwhelms him or her. This is the Baptism in the Holy Spirit. So, it is not a matter of passing the Baptism in the Holy Spirit on to others, whatever that means.

Furthermore, it is not true that only the Apostles of the Lamb could lay hands on believers to be filled with the Spirit. Those who teach this error say that Phillip, although he had led the people in Samaria to Christ, could not lay hands on them to be filled with the Holy Spirit because he was not an apostle. They say that Peter and John, who were two of the Apostles of the Lamb, had to be sent from Jerusalem to lay their hands on these new believers so that they could be filled with the Spirit. On their arrival they laid their hands on the new believers, and these got filled with the Holy Spirit. This then, they say, is passing the Baptism in the Holy Spirit on to others.

This is not the case at all. Peter and John were endowed with a gift for laying hands on believers to be filled with the Spirit. They did not get success in this regard because they were Apostles of the Lamb. How do we know that? Well, Peter, who is the Apostle of the Lamb in question, said so himself.

Acts 8:18-20 – *And when Simon saw that through the laying on of the apostles' hands the Holy Spirit was given, he offered them money, saying,*

"Give me this power also, that anyone on whom I lay hands may receive the Holy Spirit." But Peter said to him, "Your money perish with you, because you thought that the gift of God could be purchased with money!

Simon wanted to buy the power to lay hands on people to be filled with the Spirit. He did not want to buy the Holy Spirit. Peter, who understood exactly what he wanted to buy, rebuked him, saying that he could not purchase the 'gift of God'.

The gift Peter was speaking about was the power to lay hands on believers to receive the baptism in the Holy Spirit. This proves that Phillip recognized that Peter and John had a special gift in this regard and had called for them. In this way he speeded up the matter of getting people filled with the Holy Spirit.

Holding unto the position that only the Apostles of the Lamb could lay hands on believers to be filled with the Holy Spirit becomes problematic when the records in the Book of Acts are examined. Nobody laid hands on the believing people in Cornelius' home when they got filled with the Holy Spirit. The Spirit was poured out by a sovereign act of God as He had done on the Day of Pentecost (Acts 10:44-48).

Paul did not get filled with the Holy Spirit because one of the twelve Apostles of the Lamb laid hands on him. Ananias, who was simply referred to as a disciple, was sent by the Lord to lay hands on Saul (later called Paul) who went on to become a great apostle (Acts 9:17). So, the Lord also did not know about this doctrine of 'only the Apostles of the Lamb could lay hands on believers to be filled with the Holy Spirit'.

The Apostles of the Lamb were in a category of their own but there were other apostles too. Paul was one of them. Paul also administered the Baptism in the Holy Spirit to those whom he came across and those who got saved under his ministry (Acts 19:1-7; Gal. 3:5). Paul was also totally unaware of 'only the apostles of the Lamb could lay hands on people to be filled with the Spirit' doctrine.

Some just take a general position that the Baptism in the Holy Spirit and the accompanying gifts ceased after 'the last apostle' died. Their use of the term 'the last apostle' includes all apostles of that day, regardless of whether they were Apostles of the Lamb or any other class of apostle, like Paul was.

The argument of the proponents of this doctrine falls apart when the truth that there was no 'last apostle' becomes apparent from scripture. The ministry gifts of apostle, prophet, evangelist, pastor and teacher continued throughout the gospel era and are still in existence today. The scripture says that God appointed these ministry gifts in the church (1 Cor. 12:28). The church is still in existence today, and so also the ministry gifts. When Christ comes for His church at the rapture, there will be many apostles still alive on the earth.

Error: Bible is Here – Gifts are Not Needed

Teaching that the gifts of the Spirit have ceased to manifest because we now have the bible is a false doctrine. Those who peddle this error claim that, since we have the full canon of scripture, the church has all that it needs as far as divine revelation and edification are concerned.

However, the gifts of the Holy Spirit, which includes the gift of Different Kinds of Tongues, did not cease to manifest when the full canon of scripture was compiled. They have manifested throughout the ages and do so even today. Those who teach that the gifts ceased to manifest then, try to back up their argument by referring to what Paul wrote in his first letter to the Corinthians.

---

1 CORINTHIANS 13:8-10 – *Love never fails. But whether there are prophecies, they will fail; whether there are tongues, they will cease; whether there is knowledge, it will vanish away. For we know in part and we prophesy in part. But when that which is perfect has come, then that which is in part will be done away.*

They focus on the words, 'but when that which is perfect has come, then that which is in part will be done away', and conclude that the 'perfect' is the bible. They then come up with a teaching like, 'The perfect that is come is the bible, and since the bible has come, the gifts which are just a "part" have been done away with'. Despite their strong stand along these lines, a cursory reading of the scripture proves that this is a false teaching.

One has to stretch human reasoning beyond its limits to make the words 'that which is perfect' into a reference to the bible. Paul did not even know that his letters would be part of the New Testament and could never have been referring to the completion of the canon of scripture. Those who try to defend their position by saying that there was a prophetic element in Paul's words must remember that they don't apply the same rule to other scripture.

'When that which is perfect has come' refers to when we get to heaven. It must be heaven because Paul says, "For now we see in a mirror, dimly, but then face to face. Now I know in part, but then I shall know just as I also am known." Is this not a clear reference to when we are in heaven? At this present time, we see dimly. We do have the bible, yet no one can deny that we see dimly. We need illumination of scripture now, but then we will be face to face with the Lord. What need will there be for prophecy and tongues and (supernatural) knowledge in heaven? All this is by nature 'part'.

When we get to heaven, prophecy will come to an end, tongues will cease, and supernatural knowledge will vanish away. That there will be no need for tongues when we get to heaven is the clear teaching of the apostle.

Error: Tongues Only for the Infant Church

Those who teach that the gifts of the Spirit were only for the 'infant church' and are no longer needed today because the church has matured, are teaching a false doctrine. The advocates of this doctrine argue that the scripture below proves that tongues was only for the 'infant church' of the first century.

---

1 CORINTHIANS 13:11-12 – *When I was a child, I spoke as a child, I understood as a child, I thought as a child; but when I became a man, I put away childish things. For now we see in a mirror, dimly, but then face to face. Now I know in part, but then I shall know just as I also am known.*

This is our answer. Paul was not saying that tongues was a childish thing, meaning a silly or immature thing, but rather saying that which is appropriate to a child. An example of this would be certain kind of clothing styles that children wear. These are perfectly appropriate to them but there is nothing silly or immature about such clothing.

The analogy that Paul uses is a perfect one. It proves the future and not the past doing away of the gifts of the Spirit. A child continues only for a while but does not cease to exist as a person when childhood ends. The child does vanish away, but into an adult. The child is no more, but gets swallowed up in the whole, the adult. Then, as an adult, the child puts away childish (not childishly silly and immature, but childlike) things. The analogy is that, while we are still on earth, we are children, but when we get to heaven we will be adults. Tongues, which is but in part, will cease to exist then, because we would have entered into the fullness of communication with God.

Error: Progress of Modern Society

There are those who argue that secular knowledge has developed to such an extent that the gifts of the Spirit of God are no longer necessary. This error is nothing but a direct attempt to side-step the supernatural.

The proponents of this type of doctrine say that, because the canon of scripture is complete, the need for the Word of Wisdom has passed away. They hold that the plan and purpose of God has been completely mapped out in the bible and there is nothing further that can be added.

I agree that it is true that we have the full revelation of God in the bible, but everyone must also agree that we still see dimly and are dependent on God to guide us into that which is already revealed. However, the Word of Wisdom is not only for that purpose. It is also for the supernatural revealing of God's plan and purpose for our personal lives in this time. We certainly need this gift.

Intellectuals reason that, because great learning institutions have arisen with knowledge on every conceivable subject, the Word of Knowledge is no longer needed. It is a fact that the world has gained much useful knowledge over the centuries, but that is not what the Word of Knowledge is all about. The gift brings forth supernatural knowledge through visions, dreams and the voice of God of things past and present. This is given so that we can act on this information given for our benefit. Such supernatural knowledge is needed today as much as it was needed in the days when the bible was written.

The advocates of this error say that the need for Discerning of Spirits has passed away because belief in demons is a superstition that belongs to ancient society. The truth is that the church is impotent without this supernatural revealing of the spiritual world. Demonic activity has not passed away but is on the increase today. We need this gift more than ever before.

These people say that faith is the only gift that is needed today. This is usually believed because this gives them leeway to escape the supernatural. They apparently use ordinary faith and think that this is the Gift of Faith. This gift is a supernatural faith granted by the Spirit for that moment to produce miracles, like raising the dead.

To dodge the supernatural, the purveyors of false doctrine say that miracles are evident around us all the time. They point to the morning sunrise and the birth of a baby and say these are miracles. These are, of course, natural miracles, but the gift in question is the gift of Working of Miracles that multiplies fish and bread to feed the multitudes.

Again, to duck the supernatural these people say that there are top class hospitals today and that they are more than capable of helping the sick. As a result of this, the Gift of Healings is not needed today. Unfortunately, since people first began to say that, the need for hospitals has increased more than a thousandfold. Supernatural healings are needed and are still happening today.

For the sake of brevity, and in line with the above explanations, we say that Prophecy, Different Kinds of Tongues and Interpretation of Tongues are still alive and well today.

The errors discussed above are easily – and once and for all – settled by the statement Peter made on the Day of Pentecost, which should bring an end to such false doctrines for any honest seeker.

ACTS 2:38-39 – *Then Peter said to them, 'Repent, and let every one of you be baptized in the name of Jesus Christ for the remission of sins; and you shall receive the gift of the Holy Spirit. For the promise is to you and to your children, and to all who are afar off, as many as the Lord our God will call.'*

Peter said that the promise of the Baptism in the Holy Spirit and the speaking in tongues that had just been witnessed, was for those in front of him. This means that it was for that generation. He also said that it was for their children, which was the next generation. Then he said it was for 'those who were afar off'. This does not mean those who were in distant lands but the generations yet to come. Finally, he said that the promise was for 'as many as the Lord our God shall call'. This all-encompassing statement includes every succeeding generation of believers until the end of the gospel era. Enough said.

2   ERROR: THE GIFTS ARE FOR TODAY BUT…

Error: Not Every Believer Can Speak in Tongues

Teaching that not everybody will speak in tongues when they get baptized in the Holy Spirit or after that is a false teaching. Sincere people have misunderstood and misinterpreted what Paul wrote to the Corinthians. These people who teach such a doctrine have never ventured into things of the Spirit and have built up a false doctrine out of their wrong thinking.

---

1 Corinthians 12:28-30 – *And God has appointed these in the church: first apostles, second prophets, third teachers, after that miracles, then gifts of healings, helps, administrations, varieties of tongues. Are all apostles? Are all prophets? Are all teachers? Are all workers of miracles? Do all have gifts of healings? Do all speak with tongues? Do all interpret?*

Paul asks his readers several questions. In each case the answer is an obvious, "No". "There you have it," they say. "Not everybody speaks in tongues, and not everybody interprets tongues," and this ill-informed statement is supposed to reduce us to an ignominious silence. However, a simple explanation resolves the problem of the obvious "No".

The context of the scripture must be taken into consideration. Paul was speaking about the progression of ministry gifts in the church and not about the gifts of the Holy Spirit. All nine gifts of the Holy Spirit were manifest in the church from the beginning and are listed earlier in the same twelfth chapter of First Corinthians.

---

1 CORINTHIANS 12:8-10 – *for to one is given the word of wisdom through the Spirit, to another the word of knowledge through the same Spirit, to another faith by the same Spirit, to another gifts of healings by the same Spirit, to another the working of miracles, to another prophecy, to another discerning of spirits, to another different kinds of tongues, to another the interpretation of tongues.*

Gifts of the Spirit are all manifestations of the Spirit of God. For example, the Holy Spirit might manifest Himself through a Spirit-filled believer, giving that person a Word of Knowledge. This can come in the form of an inner voice, a dream or a vision. It could be a once-off manifestation through any believer or, as is in some cases, a person might have regular manifestations of the gift. These manifestations of the Spirit are for every believer because Paul says, "The manifestation of the Spirit is given to each one" (1 Cor. 12:7).

In the first scripture given above, Paul deals with ministry gifts and not gifts of the Spirit. Ministry gifts are different to gifts of the Spirit. Ministry gifts are embodied in a person. For example, one person is an apostle, another is a prophet, another is an evangelist, another is a pastor and yet another is a teacher. A ministry gift (the person) has a particular anointing and will have certain gifts of the Spirit in manifestation.

In the passage of scripture under discussion, Paul shows that there was a development of ministry gifts in the church. It was not his intention to simply list the ministry gifts, although in his argument he did leave a record for us. He says that the first ministry gift that was set in the church was the apostle. Then God added the ministry gift of the prophet to the church. Then, as the need arose, He added the ministry gift of the teacher to the church. There should be no doubt that the setting of ministry gifts in the church is the subject of Paul's discussion at this point.

An honest student will also agree that he does not digress but continues to speak about the adding of ministry gifts to the church. Miracles then must also be a ministry gift. Miracles represents the evangelist with this particular gift in manifestation. This is proven to be true because in the next verse he describes this person as 'a worker of miracles'.

Paul continues to discuss the progression of ministry gifts and lists another type of evangelist who has healing prominent in his or her life and calls this ministry gift, 'Gifts of Healings'. This is the progression: first apostles were set in place and then the prophet was set in the church, then the teacher and then the evangelist rose up as a full ministry gift.

Paul continues speaking about the setting of ministry gifts in the church. As the church developed, the ministry gift of Helps was set in place. This a ministry gift and describes the person who works on the full smooth co-ordination of a church or ministry. This person has a special anointing resident within to accomplish this.

God also added at that time Administrations to the church. This is a ministry gift, relating to the administration of a ministry. Varieties of Tongues must then also be a ministry gift that was added to the church as the church developed. Helps, Administrations, Variety of Tongues are all ministry gifts, although not on the level of the five-fold ministry, namely apostle, prophet, evangelist, pastor and teacher.

Helps and Administrations are sometimes associated with those mentioned in other scriptures (Rom. 12:6-8; 1 Pet. 4:10-11). Variety of Tongues is a special type of ministry gift.

Variety of Tongues is a ministry gift that is embodied in a person. This is a person who is endowed with an anointing whereby he or she will speak to a congregation or to someone in tongues and interpret on a regular basis. This will be on a higher level than someone who just yields from time to time. The person who operates in this ministry gift will be known for this and will be recognized as a gift to the church. The person is anointed and the Gift of Different Kinds of Tongues manifests through that person on a regular basis. Sometimes, a husband and wife who are in the ministry will operate in this ministry gift. The husband perhaps will speak in tongues as he ministers to a person and the wife will interpret, and sometimes vice versa. In a church service where people come to the front to be ministered to, the couple could continue down the line until many have been ministered to like this. This will lead to counselling by this ministry gift or the pastors of the church. Thus the needs of the congregation are met.

Now, we ask the question relating to tongues again. Does everyone have the ministry gift of speaking in tongues? The answer is obviously "No". Does everyone speak in tongues when they get baptized in the Holy Spirit? The answer is "Yes", because this is the scriptural evidence of the baptism in the Holy Spirit. Can everyone speak in tongues after they get baptized in the Spirit? The answer is "Yes", because Paul himself says, "I wish you all spoke with tongues," and, "Do not forbid to speak with tongues".

In churches where the Holy Spirit has free sway, both the gifts of the Spirit manifest and ministry gifts develop. In churches where the work of the Holy Spirit is limited, there are no practical examples that are demonstrated for people to learn from. The result is faulty exposition of the scriptures.

Error: Tongues Can Be Taught

Those who try to teach people to speak in tongues by asking them to repeat words of tongues after them, are teaching a false doctrine. This deception grows out of ignorance and a desire to get people to yield to the Holy Spirit.

---

1 CORINTHIANS 14:1 – *Now concerning spiritual gifts, brethren, I do not want you to be ignorant*

Putting this into practice produces confusion in the house of God and gives the unlearned reason to criticize those who believe in legitimate speaking in tongues. Misguided believers who desire the power of God end up discouraged.

When someone is asked to repeat words spoken in a tongue, they use their minds to memorize what has been spoken in tongues by someone else, and then they attempt to say those words. It is obvious, therefore, that the words are from the mind of that person, though unintelligible. The gullible are then told that they have spoken in tongues.

Tongues are supernatural utterances that are given by the Holy Spirit. When a Spirit-filled believer yields to the Holy Spirit, and speaks in tongues, words from the Spirit are released into the spirit of the believer, who then speaks these words out. It all happens in a micro Holy Spirit instant, but the Word of God divides it up for us to understand. It is the spirit of the believer that speaks by the help of the Holy Spirit.

---

1 CORINTHIANS 14:14 – *For if I pray in a tongue, my spirit prays, but my understanding is unfruitful.*

Every utterance in tongues is new and unique and has its own meaning. Tongues come directly from the Holy Spirit through the spirit of a believer. It does not come from the Holy Spirit through one believer and then to the mind of another and then spoken out. This is foolishness.

The Spirit-filled believer must be taught to yield to the Spirit-given utterances. A full teaching on this is given in an earlier chapter.

Error: Tongues Are Natural Abilities

Those who teach that tongues and the other gifts are natural abilities are teaching a false doctrine. All the gifts are supernatural manifestations of the Spirit of God.

---

1 CORINTHIANS 12:7 – *But the manifestation of the Spirit is given to each one for the profit of all:*

Different Kinds of Tongues are supernatural Holy Spirit-given utterances that are given through a Spirit-filled believer and they constitute languages that have never been learned and are not understood by that speaker and, in nearly all occurrences, not understood by the hearer. There is absolutely nothing natural about them and every manifestation of the gift is a vocal miracle.

Faithless and ignorant people try to sweep away the supernatural by outrageous teachings. How people can swallow such junk will amaze Spirit-filled believers who have but a rudimentary knowledge of the gifts.

---

1 JOHN 2:27 – *But the anointing which you have received from Him abides in you, and you do not need that anyone teach you; but as the same anointing teaches you concerning all things, and is true, and is not a lie, and just as it has taught you, you will abide in Him.*

Some teach that the gift of Different Kinds of Tongues is an extraordinary natural ability that is given by God so that a believer can learn foreign languages easily for the purpose of preaching the gospel to the people of those countries. This is a false doctrine designed to dismiss the supernatural nature of the gift. A flair for learning foreign languages easily is a natural ability that even unbelievers possess.

It is wonderful to listen to someone who suddenly enters an unexpected ease and freedom in anointed preaching. However, it will not be true to describe this as speaking in tongues. That would be ignorance going astray like a misguided missile and it is bound to hit the leader of the denomination squarely between the eyes.

The same type of faithless explanation is given for each gift of the Spirit. Interpretation of Tongues is taught to be a sharp gift in explaining scripture. The blessed Gift of Prophecy is called preaching. The Word of Knowledge is abbreviated to knowledge and the Word of Wisdom is a word in season. Discerning of Spirits is reduced to what is really suspicion. The Gift of Faith is equated with someone who appears to be strong in natural exploits; the Working of Miracles to natural miracles, like the birth of a child; and the Gift of Healings is given the lowly status of people having education in medical matters and who are able to help people who are sick. So, they carry on and on and on, but I say great and mighty is the Spirit of the living God.

Error: Tongues Cleansed Vocabulary

Those who teach that tongues are nothing but a cleansed Christian vocabulary are teaching a false doctrine. This us not just harmless wrong thinking to be dismissed lightly, because believing such a lie steals a lifetime of blessing from the believer. The proponents of this doctrine try to prove their stance by eliminating the supernatural from the scripture given below.

MARK 16:17-18 – *And these signs will follow those who believe: In My name they will cast out demons; they will speak with new tongues; they will take up serpents; and if they drink anything deadly, it will by no means hurt them; they will lay hands on the sick, and they will recover."*

This is what they say: "When Jesus said that believers will speak in tongues, He meant that they will have a new and clean way of speaking. No more will they swear, curse, utter profanities, tell dirty jokes and blaspheme. There will be no more lying or gossip that comes out of their mouths. Their talking will be cleansed, resulting in a 'new tongue'."

They then stand back and triumphantly add, "No corrupt communication, no salt water and no more vulgarities". This is such a weak and ignorant argument that one feels that it should be dismissed with all the contempt that it deserves. What degree of intelligence would still put forth such an argument in this day and age?

We ask the following questions. Is casting out demons not a supernatural sign? Is the protection against harm when taking up serpents and drinking poison (accidentally) not a supernatural sign? Is healing that comes from laying on of hands not a supernatural sign? The answer to each of these questions is an obvious "Yes". If this is the case – and it is – then why will 'they will speak in new tongues' be reduced to a natural outcome? It is obvious that the Lord was saying that the supernatural would follow all those who believe.

3 ERROR: TONGUES NECESSARY FOR SALVATION

Baptism in the Holy Spirit, with its scriptural evidence of speaking in other tongues, does not cause the new birth to take place in a sinner. Those who teach that it does are teaching a false doctrine. The error is not that the scriptural evidence of the baptism in the Holy Spirit is speaking in tongues, which it is, but that this baptism is what causes one to be born again.

The main reason why the advocates of this doctrine believe that a person must be baptized in the Spirit, with the evidence of speaking in tongues, in order to be born again, is because they think that the Lord Jesus was teaching this in the third chapter of the book of John.

JOHN 3:5 – *Jesus answered, 'Most assuredly, I say to you, unless one is born of water and the Spirit, he cannot enter the kingdom of God.'*

Unfortunately, they read thoughts into this scripture that are not there at all. As a result of this, they have built up a false doctrine that has deceived many. The serving of this in a legitimate piece of meat, namely 'salvation by grace, based on the atoning work of the Lord Jesus Christ', makes for easy swallowing by the unsuspecting.

The phrase 'born of water' does not refer to baptism in water. Teaching that it does and is necessary for salvation is teaching Baptismal Regeneration, which is a false doctrine. Only the blood of the Lord Jesus can wash away sins.

EPHESIANS 1:7 – *In Him we have redemption through His blood, the forgiveness of sins, according to the riches of His grace*

In the first scripture given above, the word 'water' refers to the Word of God (John 15:3; Titus 3:5) and 'born... of the Spirit' refers to the power of the Spirit to produce the new birth. These are the two operating powers in the born-again experience.

When a sinner turns away from every false hope of salvation (Acts 17:30) or from a disbelief or a disregard of God (Ps. 14:1), believes that Christ has provided full atonement for his or her sins (Rom. 3:25-26), confesses Christ Jesus as Lord (Rom. 10:9-10) and expresses that faith in action (James 2:26) the Word of God drops into that person's spirit and by the action and power of the Holy Spirit the old nature is blasted out and the Spirit causes a rebirth of that person's spirit. This is how a person gets born again.

Paul's teaching on the born-again experience lines up with the Lord's words. He wrote a letter to Titus, saying that we are saved 'through the washing of regeneration and renewing of the Holy Spirit' (Tit. 3:5). The 'washing' is a reference to the Word and the 'renewing' is the work of the Spirit in the new birth. Peter taught the same thing in his first epistle, when he wrote, "Having been born again, not of corruptible seed but incorruptible, through the word of God which lives and abides forever" (1 Pet. 1:23).

The sinner is brought into the Kingdom of God when he or she gets born again. That the born-again experience is a necessity for salvation is evidenced by the words of the Lord Jesus Christ in the first scripture given above. The Lord said that, unless a person was born again, that person would not see the kingdom of God. Those who say that the Lord was speaking about the baptism in the Holy Spirit and that unless a person is baptized in the Holy Spirit with the evidence of speaking in tongues, they cannot be saved, introduce a doctrine that is foreign to the bible.

Baptism in the Holy Spirit is a separate, distinct and subsequent experience to salvation. The born-again experience is typified by a well of water (John 4:10-14) and the baptism in the Holy Spirit by rivers of living water (John 7:37-39). The resurrected Lord breathed on the disciples, bringing about the born-again experience (John 20:22) and these same disciples received the baptism in the Holy Spirit a number of days later, on the Day of Pentecost (Acts 2:4).

Peter's instructions to those who heard him preach on the Day of Pentecost were that they first repent of rejecting Jesus Christ, and then they could receive the baptism in the Holy Spirit (Acts 2:38). The Samaritans first got saved and then hands were laid on them and they received the baptism in the Holy Spirit (Acts 8:14-17). Paul first got saved and then hands were laid on him and he was filled with the Spirit (Acts 19:17).

Cornelius and those who were at his home first heard the word (that means that they got saved), and almost simultaneously got filled with the Spirit (Acts 10:44-48). The Ephesians, in Acts, chapter nineteen, first had the gospel preached to them, and then hands were laid on them and they got filled with the Spirit (Acts 19:1-7).

Baptism in the Holy Spirit happens after a person gets born again. It is not the born-again experience. The teaching that a person must receive the baptism in the Holy Spirit with the evidence of speaking in tongues in order to be saved, is a declaration that millions of devout Christians who have died have gone to hell and those who are alive today have the same destination. How can all these people who have turned wholeheartedly to the Lord, have believed that He died and was raised from the dead, and have in all sincerity confessed and confess that He is Lord, perish in their sins? This false doctrine dismisses the clear teaching of the scriptures that we are justified by faith in the Lord Jesus Christ.

The Baptism in the Holy Spirit is for power, because the Lord Himself said that we shall receive power after the Holy Spirit has come upon us (Acts 1:8). Some born-again Christians reach out and receive it, while others delay receiving and others think that it is not for today. Notwithstanding the clear teaching of the scriptures that the promise is for all, their refusal to receive does not mean that they will perish in their sins.

HOW TO BE SAVED AND FILLED WITH THE SPIRIT

How to Get Saved

If you are not saved, then you are in grave danger of losing your eternal soul. You are a sinner and your final destination is Hell. God must send every sinner there, if he or she dies in sin. However, nobody needs to go there because the Lord Jesus Christ has paid the full price for their sins. He fully dealt with Satan and sin in His crucifixion, death, burial, resurrection, ascension and exaltation to the right hand of God the Father. He now offers the free gift of salvation to whoever wants to be saved. You can be saved. If you want to, do the following.

Turn away from every false hope of salvation, disbelief or disregard of God. Then believe that the Lord Jesus Christ has paid the price for your sin and confess Him as Lord. At the moment you do that, express your faith by thanking God that you are saved. Do this and you will be saved.

Pray the prayer that I have given you below. Do it with all sincerity and in doing so you will be doing what I have shared with you above.

The Sinners Prayer

Almighty God, I am a sinner. I have continually violated Your righteousness by refusing to submit to Your eternal rule. Hell is my final destination, if I should die in my sins. I have not only rejected Your righteous rule but, in my pursuit of sin, I have neglected the free gift of salvation. I have, I realize now with grief, dishonoured the great King of heaven and earth. My only hope is if You extend mercy to me now. If not, I will perish in the eternal sufferings of the Lake of Fire.

Almighty God, I now turn away from my rebellion. Today and right now, I turn away from every false hope of salvation, from unbelief and my disregard for You. You have directed sinners to repent and to accept the free gift of salvation that you have provided through Jesus Christ the Son of God. Please forgive me as I do so now.

I do believe that the Lord Jesus Christ died for me on the cross, suffered for me and has fully paid the price for sin. I embrace this truth with all my heart. I also confess with my own mouth that Jesus Christ is Lord. He is the Son of God.

I now lift up my hands to you, Almighty God, and utter my first hallelujah! Hallelujah!

Your Word is true, so I know that You have forgiven me and washed away my sins. I can therefore boldly declare that I am saved. Thank You for saving me.

The Baptism in the Holy Spirit

The baptism in the Holy Spirit may be received in three ways. One is by means of a sovereign move of God, another is through the laying on of hands and the other is through the prayer of faith.

Sovereign Move of God

God has supreme power and knows all things. He knows when all things are perfect and when He can pour out His Spirit on a believer. This is what is called a sovereign move of God. There is no human co-operation that is necessary when God does this. There are two records of God doing this in the Book of Acts. For the sake of brevity I will not expound on this but will leave it up to you to read and study these scriptures.

ACTS 2:1-4 – *When the Day of Pentecost had fully come, they were all with one accord in one place. And suddenly there came a sound from heaven, as of a rushing mighty wind, and it filled the whole house where they were sitting. Then there appeared to them divided tongues, as of fire, and one sat upon each of them. And they were all filled with the Holy Spirit and began to speak with other tongues, as the Spirit gave them utterance.*

ACTS 10:44-46 – *While Peter was still speaking these words, the Holy Spirit fell upon all those who heard the word. And those of the circumcision who believed were astonished, as many as came with Peter, because the gift of the Holy Spirit had been poured out on the Gentiles also. For they heard them speak with tongues and magnify God.*

Laying on of Hands

The baptism in the Holy Spirit can also be received through the laying on of hands. Some ministers have a gift to lay hands on people to receive the Baptism in the Holy Spirit like this. The scriptures prove to us that Peter, James and Paul had this gift. You can ask someone who is used by God in this particular way to lay hands on you so that you can receive the baptism in the Holy Spirit.

ACTS 8:14-19 – *Now when the apostles who were at Jerusalem heard that Samaria had received the word of God, they sent Peter and John to them, who, when they had come down, prayed for them that they might receive the Holy Spirit. For as yet He had fallen upon none of them. They had only been baptized in the name of the Lord Jesus. Then they laid hands on them, and they received the Holy Spirit. And when Simon saw that through the laying on of the apostles' hands the Holy Spirit was given, he offered them money, saying, "Give me this power also, that anyone on whom I lay hands may receive the Holy Spirit."*

ACTS 19:1-7 – *And it happened, while Apollos was at Corinth, that Paul, having passed through the upper regions, came to Ephesus. And finding some disciples he said to them, "Did you receive the Holy Spirit when you believed?" So they said to him, "We have not so much as heard whether there is a Holy Spirit." And he said to them, "Into what then were you baptized?" So they said, "Into John's baptism." Then Paul said, "John indeed baptized with a baptism of repentance, saying to the people that they should believe on Him who would come after him, that is, on Christ Jesus." When they heard this, they were baptized in the name of the Lord Jesus. And when Paul had laid hands on them, the Holy Spirit came upon them, and they spoke with tongues and prophesied. Now the men were about twelve in all.*

The Prayer of Faith

Believers may also receive the baptism in the Holy Spirit by means of the prayer of faith. The scripture below makes this clear and the steps to achieving this are set out for you.

LUKE 11:13 – *If ye then, being evil, know how to give good gifts unto your children: how much more shall your heavenly Father give the Holy Spirit to them that ask him?*

The first step to receiving the baptism in the Holy Spirit is to be saved (John 14:17). Those who are not saved cannot receive the Baptism in the Holy Spirit. If you are not saved follow the guidance, I have given you before.

Second, want and desire an Acts 2:4 experience because there is nothing else that God can give you. On the day of Pentecost, they were all filled with the Holy Spirit and began to speak with other tongues, as the Spirit gave them utterance. Read the scripture.

Third, be fully persuaded that the baptism in the Holy Spirit is the will of God for every believer throughout the gospel era. On the Day of Pentecost, Peter called all his hearers to repentance and said to them that, if they repented, they would receive the gift of the Holy Spirit. These are his words: "For the promise is to you and to your children, and to all who are afar off, as many as the Lord our God will call" (Acts 2:38-39). You can receive nothing from God unless you know that it is His will. Faith begins where the will of God is revealed.

Fourth, meditate on the above scriptures, remembering that the Lord Jesus Christ said, "If you abide in Me, and My words abide in you, you will ask what you desire, and it shall be done for you" (John 15:7). So, don't rush ahead but read all about the Baptism in the Holy Spirit in the Book of Acts.

Fifth, when you are ready, go into your prayer closet and ask the Father, in the name of Jesus Christ, to baptize you in the Holy Spirit (John 16:23-24).

Sixth, believe that your prayer has been answered. Take Him at His word and receive the Baptism in the Holy Spirt by faith. Just as you received the Son by faith, so receive the baptism by faith (Mark 11:24). Thank the Father for the baptism in the Holy Spirit.

Seventh, yield to the Holy Spirit by lifting up your voice and in faith cooperate with the Holy Spirit and speak out in tongues. When you do that, one of two things might happen. You might sense the rising up of tongues from deep within you that will overflow into a clear language as you speak. On the other hand, you might just experience a stammer of lips resulting in a few words. If this happens, just continue speaking until a clear language starts breaking forth from your spirit. This will give you confidence that you have been baptized in the Holy Spirit.

In the days that follow, when you are alone, at will yield to the Holy Spirit and speak in tongues. The scriptures direct us to do so. "What is the conclusion then? I will pray with the spirit, and I will also pray with the understanding. I will sing with the spirit, and I will also sing with the understanding" (1 Cor. 14:15).

FINAL WORD

I hope that you have read this book in its entirety and have been enriched by the revelation that has been given to us by the Holy Spirit. It is my prayer that all readers will describe its contents as, 'good measure, pressed down, shaken together and running over'. I am persuaded that this book is a power house, locked up in a few pages.

Don't just be a hearer of the Word, be a doer. If you want to experience the full benefit of the revelation that has been shared with you, you must act upon the knowledge that you have received. If you do, God will take you out of all your troubles speedily, set His plan and purpose for your life in motion, deal with the wicked one who is set against you and propel the church into greater glory. All this will be done with extraordinary speed and all to your utter amazement.

You will have noticed that each chapter is set out in such a way that you can return to any portion of the book to study each concept separately. When you go into your prayer room, take this book with you and first study a chapter or a portion of a chapter, consulting your bible all the time and the relevant scriptures that have been given throughout. After that, you can pray in tongues. If you are diligent in this, over time you will be well grounded in things pertaining to and the Holy Spirit.

Preachers and teachers of the Word will find the book an extremely useful resource, as a study tool and as a basis for messages on the power of praying at length in the tongues.

There is no doubt in my mind that more illumination of the revelation of tongues and of the other gifts of the Spirit will be given to me and will lead to more writing.

www.ingramcontent.com/pod-product-compliance
Lightning Source LLC
Chambersburg PA
CBHW022130050726
47590CB00002B/493